The A-Z of Gardening

The AZ of Gardening

Edited by Martin Parsons

Cathay Books

First published in Great Britain
by Octopus Books Ltd
This edition published by Cathay Books Ltd
59 Grosvenor Street
London W1

© 1977 Octopus Books Ltd
ISBN 0 86178 204 6

Printed in Singapore

'September Charm', a 3-ft. tall variety of Anemone hupehensis.

Achillea
Yarrow, Milfoil (Hardy Perennial)
This genus of 200 plants includes a few good and showy plants, but also some of a weedy nature. All have flowers useful for cutting. They flower in spring and early summer and possess beauty both of leaf and flower. They are easily grown in any well-drained soil. *A. fili-pendulina* with plate-like heads of deep yellow on erect 4-ft. stems is deservedly popular. It needs the minimum of attention and is usually offered under the name 'Gold Plate'. Stems cut at their best can be dried for winter decoration. *A.* 'Moonshine', 18 in., canary-yellow with silvery leaves, flowers from May to July. *A. millefolium* is deep pink, and almost red variants, such as 'Cerise Queen' make quite a brave show before they need curbing. All should be divided in early autumn or spring. Many plants are suitable for the rock garden. The following are unlikely to exceed 6 in. when in flower. *A. argentea* has intensely silver leaves and white flowers; *A. chrysocoma* has grey leaves and yellow flowers; *A.* 'King Edward' has soft grey-green leaves and lemon yellow flowers, *A. tomentosa* green leaves and bright yellow flowers, *A. ptarmica* daisy-like white flowers.

Anemone
Windflower (Hardy Perennial)
A. hupehensis (long known as *A. japonica*) can contribute much to the late summer display. Shades of pink and white are the only colours. Individual flowers ranging from $1\frac{1}{2}$–3 in. across are like dog roses, with yellow-stamened centres. The wiry, branching stems are tipped by nodding flowers and close-set buds. Most varieties begin flowering in late July or early August and will continue until autumn. They need good drainage and a mainly sunny position and they are especially good on chalky soil. The spring flowering species have large flowers, on 8–12-in. stems, in bright red, violet, lavender and purple, some shaded with white, single in De Caen varieties and semi-double in St. Brigid. In mild districts plant the tubers at any time; elsewhere put in in April, June and September. They require rich, moist, well-cultivated soil. Protect plants intended for winter flowering by cloches or frames. *A. blanda* has little tubers. Soak the tubers before planting in autumn $1\frac{1}{2}$ in. deep in a sunny position, or under deciduous shrubs pruned off the ground. White, pink, blue, violet and carmine forms occur. Several species are admirable rock garden plants. They like well-drained, gritty soil, which is rich in humus and are increased by division or by seeds.

Annuals for Special Purposes
Hardy annuals for Autumn sowing in the open
Alyssum, Calendula (pot marigold), Centaurea (cornflower), Clarkia, *Delphinium ajacis* (larkspur), Eschscholzia (Californian poppy), Godetia, Iberis (Candytuft), *Lathyrus odoratus* (sweet pea), *Limnanthes douglasii*, Nigella (love-in-a-mist), *Papaver nudicaule* (Shirley poppy), Saponaria, Scabiosa.
Hardy Annuals for Cut Flowers
Calendula (pot marigold), Centaurea (cornflower), *Delphinium ajacis* (larkspur), Gypsophila, *Lathyrus odoratus* (sweet pea), Nigella (love-in-a-mist), Saponaria, Scabiosa.

Annuals for Full Sun in Well-drained soil
(Hardy and Half-hardy)
Arctotis, Brachycome, Calandrinia, Clarkia, Dimorphotheca, Echium, Eschscholzia, Helipterum, Hibiscus, Linum (flax), Mesembryanthemum, Oenothera, Papaver (poppy), Portulaca, Salpiglossis, Sanvitalia, Sedum (stonecrop), Statice (limonium), Tagetes (African and French marigolds), Tropaeolum (nasturtium), Ursinia, Venidium, Zinnia.

Annual Climbers
Cobaea scandens, Eccremocarpus scaber, Gourds, Humulus (hop), *Ipomoea* (morning glory), *Lathyrus odoratus* (sweet pea), Maurandia, Quamoclit, Tropaeolum (nasturtium).

Left: Achillea filipendulina 'Gold Plate'

Right: Anemone apennina should be planted in early March

Annuals with Fragrant Flowers

Alyssum, Asperula, Centaurea (sweet sultan), Dianthus (pink), Exacum, Heliotrope (cherry pie), Hesperis (sweet rocket), *Lathyrus odoratus* (sweet pea), *Lupinus luteus* (yellow lupin), Matthiola (stocks), Nicotiana (tobacco plant), Oenothera (evening primrose), Reseda (mignonette), Tropaeolum (nasturtium) (Gleam hybrids).

Low-growing Annuals

(from 9-18 in.)

Adonis, Anthemis, Centaurea (cornflower, dwarf forms), Collinsia, *Convolvulus tricolor*, *Coreopsis coronata*, *Coreopsis tinctoria*, Dimorphotheca, Eschscholzia, Gilia, Godetia (dwarf forms), Helipterum, Iberis (candytuft), Linaria, *Matthiola bicornis* (night-scented stock), Matthiola (ten-week stock), Omphalodes, Reseda (mignonette), Scabiosa (dwarf forms), *Tagetes patula* (dwarf French marigold), Ursinia.

Annuals for Moist Soil

Calendula (pot marigold), Helianthus (sunflower), *Limnanthes douglasii*, Linaria (toadflax), *Linum grandiflorum rubrum* (scarlet flax), Nemophila, Nigella (love-in-a-mist), Reseda (mignonette), *Saxifraga cymbalaria*.

Hardy Annuals

A hardy annual is a plant that is raised from seed, flowers, and dies a natural death within the four seasons.

Half-hardy Annuals

These are usually raised from seed sown under glass and the seedlings planted out where they are to flower when the danger of frost is past.

Biennials

A biennial is sown one year, produces its flowers and dies the following year.

Perennials

A perennial is a plant of any kind that lives for more than two years. It may be perennial in a greenhouse, others grown in the open are known as hardy perennials.

Cultivation

Hardy Annuals

Seed of hardy annuals may be sown in the open ground where they are to flower; it is as easy as that. The main requirements are an open sunny position and a well-drained soil. Obviously the condition of the soil will be reflected in the quality of the flowers produced and to get the best results fork over the ground a few days before sowing.

Before sowing rake the soil level, removing large stones and hard lumps of earth. Most flower seed is small and does need a reasonably fine surface soil in which to germinate. Sow the seed broadcast or in drills and in any case sow thinly for germination of annual flower seed is usually good. This will reduce the wasteful job of thinning. Pelleted seeds make small seeds much easier to handle and thin sowing is easily achieved.

Do not attempt to sow seed when the soil is wet and sticky. Be patient and

*Right: The most decorative
variety of the annual corn
cockle is* Agrostemma '*Milas*'

*Below: Petunia hybrids make a
bright show in summer*

*Above: Some of the
eschscholzias or Californian
poppies*

*Left: Choose a sunny position
for the colourful South African
gazanias*

wait until it dries out. Seed sowing is controlled by the weather not by the calendar. After the seed has been sown cover it lightly with soil and water, with a fine rose, just sufficiently to make the surface soil moist. Cloches are certainly useful to assist germination.

Where thinning of seedlings is necessary this should be done when they are about 2–3 in. high and a final thinning should leave sufficient space for the plants to develop.

Half-hardy Annuals

Many plants which we call half-hardy annuals are natives of much warmer lands where frost is unknown or a rare occurrence. Some are perennial in their native conditions. We must often encourage such seed to germinate with the aid of artificial heat in a greenhouse or frame. Some half-hardy annuals may be sown in the open in May or early June where they are to flower. Seeds of half-hardy annuals are sown in pots or boxes containing seed compost which is readily obtained these days in polythene bags at garden centres. It is moist and ready for use, which saves considerable time. Fill the container to within about $\frac{1}{2}$in. of the top and press the compost down evenly. Sow the seed sparsely, then sprinkle a fine covering of compost over the seed and cover the container with a piece of glass, and a sheet of brown paper as shading. The compost should not require watering at this stage as it only needs to be moist. Remove the glass daily, wiping off the condensed moisture and reverse the glass when you replace it. When the seed germinates remove the glass and paper and put the container in full light in the greenhouse or frame.

When the seedlings are large enough to handle, that is usually by the time they have developed two pairs of leaves, lift them carefully by levering up the soil with a dibber and prick them out into another box, spacing them about 2 in. apart. Plant them firmly and water them into the compost. Keep them growing steadily under glass until the beginning of May. Then, if the weather is reasonably mild, stand the boxes in the open for a week or so to harden the plants before they are planted out where they are to flower. If the boxes have been in a frame it is a simple matter of just removing the frame light for this hardening-off process. Give the boxes a good watering an hour or two before transplanting the seedlings so that they can be removed from the boxes with plenty of moist soil attached to their roots. Water them again when they are planted out.

Biennials

Seed of biennial plants may be sown straight into a seed bed in the open ground in June, July or August. As the soil is warm germination is not delayed, provided the seed bed is kept moist. Another method is to sow in drills in a cold frame in March or April, or where only a small quantity of plants is required, to sow in pots or boxes in a cold frame or cold greenhouse. Whichever method is used, sow thinly and do not make the common mistake of covering the seed with too much soil.

As a general rule cover the seed with its own depth of soil.

The Uses of Annuals and Biennials
Beds and Borders
Annuals are probably most widely used for filling gaps in borders, on the rock garden and elsewhere, for they provide splashes of welcome colour in a matter of months.
New Gardens
One of the quickest ways of making a display in a new garden is by sowing hardy annuals, for seed sown in April where it is to flower will give a display from June onwards.
Containers
For those whose gardening may be confined to window boxes, tubs or other containers on a roof garden or in a patio, half-hardy annuals are probably the best bet.
Edging and Paving
Other uses of annuals are as dwarf edging plants for the front of a bed or border, or for sowing in crevices in paving. Among these is the low-growing *Limnanthes douglasii* with quite large white flowers with a yellow centre, which seeds itself without becoming a nuisance, mesembryanthemum with gay daisy-like flowers that thrives in well-drained soil and full sun, anagallis (pimpernel), and the creeping zinnia, *Sanvitalia procumbens*, with single yellow flowers with a black centre on 6-in. stems. This curious little plant is like a miniature sunflower and never fails to attract interest.
Cut Flowers
Annuals provide a splendid selection of flowers for cutting and with a little planning flowers can be available over a long period. By sowing hardy annuals in the open in the autumn and making another sowing in the open in the spring a succession of welcome flowers will be assured.

Antirrhinum
Snapdragon (Half-hardy Annual)
9 in.–3 ft.
These long-flowering plants are usually treated as annuals although in mild districts they are short-lived perennials. For bedding purposes seed is sown in boxes or pots in a warm greenhouse in February or March. Sturdy plants should be ready for planting out in a sunny bed by mid-May. Seed may be sown in the open ground in April for flowering in late summer, but these cannot be compared with plants raised under glass. The range of colour includes crimson, pink, orange-scarlet, yellow and white, and many subtle variations. The dwarf varieties are admirable for the front of a border or for window boxes and the taller varieties are useful for cut flowers. There is also a good selection of rust-resistant hybrids, which are advised where this disease is prevalent.

Above left: Nemesias are available in many colours

Below: Apple 'Worcester Pearmain'

Apples
All tree fruits need to be staked on planting and those on dwarfing root-stock will need support for the whole of their life.

If a single vertical stake is to be used, this should be inserted before planting to obviate root damage. Some growers prefer a longer, oblique stake which is inserted at an angle of about 45° and pointing towards the prevailing wind. Such a stake must be long enough to cross the tree's trunk just below the lowest branches. Another method is to drive in two vertical stakes, one each side of the tree and at least a foot apart, then fix a crosspiece to these to which the stem will be fastened.

Apple or pear trees to be grown as oblique cordons require a system of horizontal wires. Preferably these should run from south to north and be 2, 4 and 6 ft. above the ground. Use gauge 12 galvanized wire and insert an adjustable straining bolt at one end of each wire to keep it taut. The end posts must be really stout (concrete, or angle iron posts are often used) and should have angle struts facing down the row to take the strain. Whether grown in

the open or against a wall, fan-trained trees will require a system of horizontal wires about 6 in. apart.

These preparations completed, planting may be carried out, providing that the soil is quite friable.

Dig a planting hole wide and deep enough for the roots of the tree, bush or cane to be spread out to their natural length. Clip off with the secateurs any damaged roots and shorten any one root which is substantially longer and stronger than the rest. Break up the soil at the bottom of the hole with a fork and draw in a little topsoil to form a slight mound at the centre so that the tree 'sits' on this. At this stage of the proceedings, an assistant to hold the tree is most helpful. When planting is completed and the soil firmed down, the tree should be at the same depth as it was in the nursery (the soil mark on the stem will probably be visible).

Where tree fruits which do not grow on their own roots are concerned, it is essential that the join (known as the 'union') between the top part (the 'scion') and the rootstock should be quite clear of the soil, at least 4 in. above it.

Now, your helper holding the tree at the right depth (a stick laid across the planting hole will indicate the final soil level), begin to replace the topsoil round the roots. A little moist peat mixed with this soil as you proceed will aid rapid new root growth. Never add manure. Use your fingers to work the soil well in beneath and around every root. Firm it occasionally as you work. When ground level is reached firm with your feet and then just rake over the surface.

Finally, spread over the root area a 2-in. deep mulch of rotted manure, compost or peat to preserve moisture in spring.

Immediately after planting fasten the tree temporarily to its stake. Permanent fastening should only be done a few months later when the soil has had time to settle. Inspect and adjust the fastenings of all newly-planted trees frequently in their early years. Patent plastic straps are excellent for fastening fruit trees because these incorporate a plastic buffer which prevents the stem from chafing against the stake and because they are so easily adjustable as the tree grows. Alternatively, use soft string for tying a newly-planted tree, first wrapping a piece of sacking,

old rubber inner tube or something similar round the bark.

Cordons should be tied with soft string or plastic tying tape to canes which, in turn, are tied to the horizontal wires. Similarly, espaliers and fan-trained trees should have their 'arms' tied to canes which are then fastened to the wires.

Oblique cordons should be planted at an angle of 45°, pointing to the north and with the scion part of the union on top of the rootstock part so that when the tree is bent down to a more acute angle this will tend to press the two parts of the union together rather than tear them apart.

The Care of Apples

Most gardeners plant two- or three-year-old trees which have already been pruned by the nurseryman into the required shape – bush, cordon, pyramid, espalier or fan. It is more interesting to start with a one-year-old tree (a 'maiden') and carry out the shaping yourself: this is cheaper, but it means you have to wait longer before you can pick fruit.

As soon as a new tree has been planted you must consider what pruning is necessary, according to the age of the tree. Winter pruning, carried out while the tree is dormant, promotes growth and in the early years, when the framework of the tree is being built up, can be fairly drastic. Later, when the branches to carry the crop have been developed, winter pruning should be more restrained, the aim now being to stimulate fruit bud formation rather than much more growth. Summer pruning encourages fruit bud formation and keeps trees within bounds.

Pruning Bush Trees

First Winter If a maiden has been planted, the first pruning consists of beheading it at a point immediately above a growth bud about 18 to 24 in. above soil level. This cut determines the length of stem below the main branches.

Second Winter Select the three or four sturdiest of the resultant shoots made during the first summer. These should be evenly spaced round the tree and will form the main branches from which other branches will spring. The aim should be a goblet shape with an open centre. Shorten each of the selected branches to between a third and a half of its length, making the cut beyond and close to a bud pointing to the

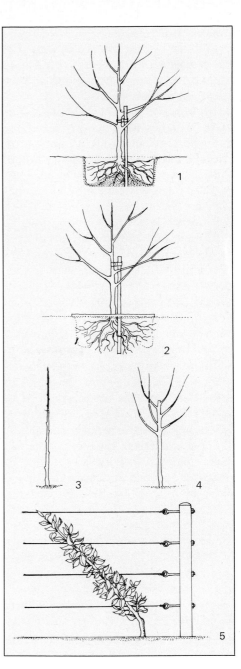

1: On heavy soil particularly, it is advisable to plant fruit trees on a mound of soil in the centre of the planting hole, as shown. 2: A stick laid across the rim of the planting hole will enable you to ensure that the tree is planted at the right depth, according to the soil mark on the stem. 3: A maiden tree is beheaded above a growth bud, about 1½–2 ft. above the ground, during the first winter after planting. 4: Branches will develop and these should be shortened during the second winter, as indicated. 5: The system of wires, posts and straining bolts used for cordon and espalier trained fruit trees

desired direction.

Cut back any other shoots, not needed as main branches, according to vigour, the weakest to one bud and the strongest to five buds.

Third Winter Each of the three or four main branches will have produced one extension growth and a number of laterals. Cut back the leader by a half. Choose two or three of the strongest and best-placed laterals as new branches and cut these, too, back by half. Cut back other laterals over 5 in. long to the fourth bud and any laterals pruned in the second winter to one bud of the new growth. Any feathers (side shoots) growing from the main stem of the tree should be removed entirely.

Fourth Winter The stage has now been reached when, to encourage fruit production, pruning may be substantially less drastic. Subsequent treatment will depend upon the habit of growth of the tree in question. Most apples form fruiting spurs naturally or when their laterals are cut hard back.

Some varieties, however, tend to make their fruit buds at the tips of young shoots and at or near the tips of older shoots. If tip-bearing varieties have all their leaders and laterals cut back, few if any fruit buds will be formed. For the spur-forming majority of varieties only tip the leaders, removing about 2 in. and cut back new laterals to three buds and previously pruned laterals to one bud of new wood. Eventually the spur systems will become overlong and possibly congested. Remove a few entirely and shorten others by a half. Should growth be weak cut back branch leaders more than usual – by a half, even three-quarters of the new growth.

Pruning Oblique Cordons

First Winter If a maiden spur-bearer is planted, no winter pruning is necessary. Prune tip-bearers back by a quarter. Cut back to three buds any feathers more than 4 in.

Mid-July Cut back mature laterals (those which are becoming woody at the base and are more than 9 in. long) to the third leaf after the basal cluster. Leave immature laterals for similar treatment mid-September. If by mid-September there has been secondary growth from your first cuts, prune this back to one bud from the point of origin.

Second July and Subsequent Years Cut back mature laterals as in previous summer. Where sub-laterals have formed,

and are mature, cut back to one leaf after the basal cluster. Deal with previously immature laterals and sub-laterals in September.

The leader of a cordon does not usually need to be cut until further height has to be restricted and then it should be shortened, as necessary, in May. Before that, however, greater length can be accommodated by unfastening the cane to which the tree is tied and pressing it down to a more acute angle before refastening to the wires.

Pruning Dwarf Pyramids

The laterals and sub-laterals along the branches of a pyramid are pruned in summer in the same way as those on cordons and, accordingly, the spur-bearing varieties are much easier to deal with than those inclined to tip-bearing.

First Winter Behead the maiden at about 20 in. above soil level, just above a bud which will grow to provide further upward extension. Rub out the next bud below this (its growth would tend to compete with the leader). The next three or four buds should point out evenly round the stem. Rub out any buds pointing in the wrong direction (i.e. too close to their neighbour). The aim is a central leader growing vertically with three or four branches evenly spaced below it. The bottom three of these buds will be stimulated if you take a notch out of the bark immediately above each bud (see definitions). Feathers more than 9 in. from the ground but less than 12 may be used to form the first branches: cut them back to about 6 in., to a bud pointing downwards.

First Summer Tie the leader to a bamboo cane if necessary to make it grow vertically. If more than four sideshoots have appeared, cut the surplus back to four leaves after the basal cluster in mid-July.

Second Winter Pruning now is designed to provide a second tier of branches to fill the gaps between the

branches of the tier below.

Cut the central leader to a bud 12 to 18 in. above the previous winter's cut and, to keep the central stem vertical, on the opposite side. Select suitable buds to form the branches, rubbing out unwanted ones and notching the two lowest. Prune back the leaders of the first tier of branches to downward-pointing buds about 9 in. from the point of origin.

Second Summer and Subsequent Years Treat laterals and sub-laterals as those on a cordon.

Third Winter Prune as in second winter. When the desired height limit has been reached defer pruning of the central leader until May and then cut it back by half. Thereafter cut new growth back to $\frac{1}{2}$ in.

Pruning Espaliers

Espaliers are usually sold ready-trained with two or three pairs of horizontal branches. There is no reason, however, why you should not plant a maiden tree and train your own espalier. Then you can have a single pair of branches or, if you wish, four, five or more tiers.

There is no rule as to the height of the first pair of branches or the space between subsequent tiers – usually about 15 in. is convenient. For preference plant an unfeathered maiden and cut back to a bud just above the lowest horizontal support wire. This bud will provide vertical growth to carry the second tier of branches 15 in. higher in a year's time. Below the top bud look for a pair of buds as nearly as possible opposite each other. The growths from these will form the lowest pair of horizontal branches and to stimulate the lowest bud make a small notch just above it. Rub out any unwanted buds.

Tie the resultant shoots from the two lower buds to canes fastened to the wires at an angle of 45°. If one shoot grows more strongly than the other, lower it slightly to a more acute angle and raise its partner slightly, nearer to the vertical. Try thus to get equal growth in the two shoots. At the end of the first season lower both canes half way to the horizontal, then down to their permanent horizontal position at the end of the second season.

Treat any laterals and sub-laterals arising from these horizontal branches as those on a cordon. Year by year a

Right: Apple 'Ellison's Orange Pippin'

further pair of new branches can be made as desired. Leaders need not be pruned until the limit of available space is reached unless growth is unsatisfactory – in which case in winter cut back the new growth of leaders.

Pruning Fans

Except in the coldest districts, apples are not satisfactory when trained against a wall. However, an apple can be fan-trained, the ribs of the fan being fastened to horizontal wires. The initial training follows the method adopted with peaches (see peaches). Once established treat each rib as if it were a cordon.

Fruit Thinning

In good years failure to thin may result in a glut of undersized apples and put such a strain on the tree that it can produce little fruit the next year. In this way a habit of biennial bearing may be induced. Certain varieties are notorious for this alternate good and bad crop habit. Timely fruit thinning will often check a tendency towards biennial bearing. Start thinning as soon as the fruitlets have set and you can form an idea of the possible crop.

With most varieties the central apple in each cluster (usually larger and hence known as the king) does not in the end prove the best. So begin by removing any obviously blemished fruitlets and then all the kings (an exception here being 'Worcester Pearmain'). Thin in about three stages, first reducing each cluster to one apple. Then continue until finally about one fruit remains for every 25 to 30 leaves. Dessert varieties should not be closer than 4 in. apart, cookers 6 in.

Watering

Never wait until signs of distress are noticeable. Watering is particularly desirable in the spring for newly-planted and young trees and an equable moisture supply in the soil is always important.

Mulch trees in early spring with a 2-in. layer of rotted manure, garden compost or peat.

Picking

An apple is ready for picking as soon as it will easily part company with the tree, the stalk remaining on the apple. Pick by taking an apple in the palm of the hand, lift it to a horizontal position and give a very slight twist. If ready, the apple will come away quite easily. The picking season begins in late July and extends into November for late

Above: A six-year-old fan-trained apple 'Sunset'

Above right: Apple 'Ellison's Orange', espalier trained, on M.7 rootstock

kinds. Early varieties of apple should be eaten quite soon after picking.

Storing

Mid-season and late apples will only keep to their proper season (by which time only will their full flavour have developed) if they have not been picked too soon (which results in premature shrivelling) and if they have been stored in good atmospheric conditions and a low temperature. A cellar provides the nearest to ideal conditions – moist air, adequate ventilation, darkness and an even temperature as near as possible to 40°F (4.5°C). If a shed has to be used, do not worry about an occasional drop in temperature to a few degrees below freezing but never handle the apples at such a time.

If you have a cellar or an insulated hut or shed, space the apples out, stalk uppermost on clean shelves. If space is short, wrap the apples separately in squares of newspaper or oiled apple wraps and put carefully into boxes.

Feeding

Where apples have been planted on cultivated garden soil of reasonable fertility they are likely to need little feeding in their early years beyond an annual spring mulch of rotted manure or compost.

Always watch for signs of potash deficiency: fruits may drop excessively or be small, leaves may assume a bluish-green shade, developing paleness between the veins and eventually looking scorched at the edges. Dress with 1 oz. per sq. yd. of sulphate of potash.

In normal circumstances a suitable

annual spring fertilizer dressing for established trees would be ½ oz. of superphosphate and ¾ oz. of sulphate of potash per sq. yd. If no natural manure or compost is available for mulching, use peat and add 1 oz. per sq. yd. of sulphate of ammonia to the fertilizer.

Over-vigorous growth can be checked by sowing fine grasses up to within a foot or so of the trunk. Mow the grass several times during the growing season but always leave the mowings to rot *in situ*. When growth has steadied down the grass will need feeding with an annual dose of 2–4 oz. of sulphate of ammonia and ½–1 oz. of sulphate of potash with ½ oz. of superphosphate per sq. yd.

Rootstocks for Apples

M.9 Most dwarfing of all. A good stock for cordons and dwarf bushes. Usually too dwarfing for espaliers and pyramids.

M.26 Less dwarfing than M.9. For small espaliers, dwarf pyramids and for cordons and dwarf bushes where soil is not rich.

M.7 and MM.106 Semi-dwarfing, producing trees of moderate size on good soil, often used for pyramids. Will produce dwarf trees on poorish soil. Recommended for cordons or varieties which do not spur freely.

M.2 and MM.111 Vigorous stocks which make big trees on good soil. May be used for espaliers where there is plenty of space and good for cordons and pyramids where the soil is definitely poor.

Notes The letters refer to the research stations originally responsible for them. M = Malling; MM = Malling-Merton. If, in a nurseryman's catalogue, a rootstock number is followed by the letter 'A', it means that the stock is from virus-tested material.

Aquilegia

Columbine (Hardy Perennial)

Very few aquilegias will come true from seed; for those who like a good range of colour and large, long-spurred flowers, such strains as 'McKana Hybrids', about 3 ft. high, and 'Beidermeier', 20 in. high, are delightful for a year or two, until replacements are needed. They are not fussy plants, and some will grow in shade. Some are good rock garden plants. They like sun and well-drained soil and flower in spring and early summer. *A. ecalcarata* has flights of elegant red-purple, spurless flowers on stems 9 in. tall. It comes true from seed; in *A. flabellata*, 9–12 in. tall, the large flowers may be blue or ivory-white; *A. glandulosa* has large blue and white flowers on 15-in. stems.

Artichoke

Artichoke (Globe) A decorative, grey-leaved thistle-like plant, this grows 4–6 ft. tall. Plants can be raised from seed but superior varieties such as 'Vert de Laon' and 'Grand Vert de Camus' are propagated from suckers. Cut flower buds for use before the bud scales are fully open.

Artichoke (Jerusalem) This hardy perennial resembles a sunflower plant and reaches a height of 10 ft. Plant tubers 1 ft. apart and 6 in. deep, in February. Lift roots as and when tubers are wanted in the kitchen between November and February.

Asparagus

(Hardy Perennial)

Plant two-year-old plants in April. 'Superior' is a new, recommended F_1 hybrid. Set plants on a ridge at the bottom of a 9-in. deep trench so that the crowns are 5 in. below the soil surface. Apply a 1-in. thick mulch of compost to the bed each spring. Do not

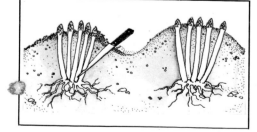

Above: Cut asparagus shoots well below soil level

Right: Aster 'Carnival' adds colour to autumn displays

harvest asparagus until the second season and when plants are well established. Sever the thick shoots well below soil level, using a sharp knife, during May and early June. Allow the foliage to grow naturally all summer but cut it down in late October.

Asparagus Ferns Invaluable for cutting and make attractive pot plants. They are not real ferns, but belong to the lily family. Use a compost such as J.I.P. 1 and keep the plants well watered, or the foliage becomes discoloured. Sow seed in spring or summer in a temperature of 60°F (16°C). Move the seedlings to 3-in. pots, discarding those of slow or irregular growth.

A. plumosus nanus has long trails of fine foliage, ideal for cutting and useful for making up buttonholes in conjunction with various flowers. *A. sprengeri* is valuable for hanging baskets as it produces sprays 1–2½ ft. long.

Aster

Callistephus, China Aster

(Half-hardy Annual)

(See also Aster, under Michaelmas Daisy) 1–2½ ft.

The diverse and colourful modern asters have been developed from *C. chinenis* but some seedsmen find they are better known as asters – not to be confused with the perennial Michaelmas daisies. Seed should be sown in a cool greenhouse in March or April, or in a sheltered garden in the open ground in early May. There are both double and single flowers and the colour range is very wide. Seedlings transplant quite readily when small. Grown *en masse* they make a splendid show in late summer and early autumn. The short-growing varieties make bushy, decorative plants in window boxes. 'Ostrich Plume', and 'Princess', both 2 ft., are admirable for cutting.

Astilbe

Saxifragaceae

Astilbes thrive in good moist soil. They have attractive foliage and the plumed flower spikes are in every imaginable shade from white through pink, salmon and cerise to fiery red and deep red. Some are erect, others arch and droop, and heights vary from 6 in. to 6 ft. They do not need staking, are completely hardy and can be left alone for years, trouble-free and reliable, though they cannot stand hot, dry conditions. They appreciate a spring mulch to conserve moisture, and they can safely be divided when dormant. In general, the tallest astilbes are the strongest and least fussy about moisture. One of the best of the taller kinds is *A. taquetii superba*, about 4 ft. with straight imposing spikes of an intense lilac-purple shade, in July and August. *A. davidii*, lilac-rose, and the varieties 'Tamarix', 'Salland', 'Venus', pale pink, and 'Salmon Queen' are all tall and robust. Given the right conditions, the more colourful dwarfer hybrid astilbes, 1½–3 ft. tall, will flower for much longer, between late June and mid-August. There are a few dwarf astilbes for cool, semi-shaded positions. Propagate by division of old plants. *A. chinensis* 'Pumila', 9–12 in., has stiff, dense spires of flowers the colour of crushed raspberries, in August and September; *A. glaberrima* 'Saxosa' has dainty spikes of pink flowers on very short stems in late summer.

Astilbes do best in moist soil

Beans

(1) *Broad Bean*   This is the only hardy garden bean. Most broad beans are tall growers. There is one true dwarf – 'The Sutton'.

When to Sow

November   Give cloche protection in colder areas. Elsewhere protect rows with small mesh chicken wire or with nylon netting to deter birds.

February   Sow single seeds in 3½-in. pots in a warm greenhouse. Peat pots are excellent for this sowing. Set plants outdoors in April – preferably with cloche protection.

March/early April   Outdoors where plants are to grow.

How to Sow

Use a draw hoe to make an 8-in. wide, 1½–2-in. deep furrow. Sow seeds in a double staggered way (see diagram) at 9 in. apart. Sow a few seeds quite close together at the end of the row; the seedlings may come in handy should any seeds in the row fail to germinate. The dwarf 'The Sutton' needs less space and seeds may be sown 6 in. apart. Leave 2½–3 ft. between rows of tall varieties and 18 in. between rows of 'The Sutton'.

Pot-raised plants should be set at these distances at planting out time.

Cultivation

Keep the plants free from weeds by hoeing. Water often and generously in warm, dry weather. Bean plants, particularly broad beans, are prone to an attack of black bean aphis. This pest favours bean plants which are short of moisture.

As well as watering when necessary, thwart black bean aphis by:

(1) Sowing in late autumn or in February; early sowings usually miss an aphis attack.

(2) Pinching out the growing point as soon as flowers have set and small pods are forming.

(3) Cutting off all tender young shoots around the base of plant.

(4) Spraying with soapy water, derris or pyrethrum in May before aphids appear.

Continue spraying weekly. Spray in the late evening so that bees are not harmed. Do not spray at all if you see ladybird larvae devouring the aphids.

(5) Destroying any weeds which harbour the aphis. Docks and fat hen are often infested with it.

In very exposed areas it helps to give tall growers supports of some kind so that plants are not blown down when cropping.

Harvest broad beans when the pods are well filled but before the seeds inside them are leathery and tough.

A typical 'Longpod' variety of broad bean

(2) *French Beans*

There are two forms – dwarf bush and climbing. The bush form is the most popular. Although the pods of most varieties are green some bear yellow or mauve pods.

When to Sow   At any time between late April and early June. It is advisable to pre-warm the soil with cloches if sowing in April. Just leave cloches in position over the soil for a week or so. Then sow and cover with cloches. Keep cloches in position for as long as possible.

Seeds may also be sown in small pots in a warm greenhouse during April. The plants must not be set out in the open garden until all risk of a late spring frost has passed.

How to Sow   Sow dwarf bush kinds as if they were broad beans. Sow climbing kinds in a single row allowing 6 in. between seeds in the row. Set out pot-raised plants at these distances. Leave 3 ft. between rows of dwarf beans; 5 ft. between rows of climbers.

Cultivation Keep down weeds and water often and well in dry weather from May onwards. Healthy plants are seldom attacked by black bean aphis. Spray with soapy water, derris or pyrethrum should this pest appear on the undersides of the leaves. If dwarf plants topple under the weight of crop, push brushwood alongside the plants to support them. Alternatively, provide strings tied to short bamboo canes. Climbing French beans attain a height of about 4 ft. Tall brushwood was the traditional form of support. Plastic garden mesh or wire mesh or plastic mesh fencing are modern supports.

Harvest French beans before the pods toughen. Pick pods often and when of full size. Cropping continues over a period of about six weeks.

(3) Runner Beans

Most runner beans bear scarlet flowers; a few have white flowers and the seeds are white. The flowers of 'Painted Lady' are red and white.

When to Sow Sow between early May and mid-June in the open garden. A sowing in April may be made under cloches. Seeds may also be sown in pots in a warm greenhouse during April. The tender plants must not be set out in the open garden until all danger of frost has passed.

How to Sow The two dwarf 'runner' beans – 'Hammond's Dwarf Scarlet' and 'Hammond's Dwarf White' – are sown and cultivated as dwarf French beans. Other varieties may be grown in two different ways. The best method is to provide the plants with tall supports. These may be traditional bean poles or bean netting. Plastic or wire fencing is also suitable. In very windy gardens runner beans may be grown as dwarfed plants.

Where plants are to have supports sow seeds at from 6 to 8 in. alongside them in a 1½–2 in. narrow furrow made with a draw hoe. If plants are to be dwarfed, sow as for broad beans. Leave from 4–5 ft. between rows of runner beans. Pot-raised plants should be set out at these distances.

Below: French bean, 'Mont D'Or', a dwarf bush variety

Cultivation Hoe to prevent weeds and water well and often in dry weather. Spray with soapy water, derris or pyrethrum should black bean aphis show on the stems or on the undersides of the leaves. Permit plants on supports to reach the top. Then pinch out the growing point at the top of each plant.

Plants to be grown dwarfed are pinched back by a few inches when the plants are 1 ft. or so high. Lots of side growths are then made. Nip these back occasionally until the row of bean plants resembles a low, bushy hedge. Support them with brushwood or with strings tied to bamboo canes. Soil which is enriched with manure or garden compost periodically is suitable. Where the

Above: Training runner beans (1) The 'standard' method: place bean 'poles' on each side of a double row of beans. (2) grow the plants up strings or netting. Where space in the vegetable garden is limited, the plants may be grown up a 'wigwam' (3) of strings or stakes, surrounding a central support

soil is not highly fertile plants may be fed with very weak liquid manure.

Harvest pods often and when they are young and tender. Never allow seeds inside the pods to plump up. Cropping should continue for two months.

(4) Beans (Haricot)

A small white haricot such as 'Comtesse de Chambord' is sown and grown as French dwarf beans. For large haricots choose 'White Wonder' and sow and cultivate as scarlet runner beans. Allow pods to remain on the plants until late summer or early autumn. After harvesting the dry pods place them in a sunny position to ripen off.

Beetroot

Beets may be round, cylindrical or long. Quick-to-mature beets for summer salads are round. 'Crimson Globe' is an example. Newer is 'Boltardy'. 'Spangsbjerg Cylinder' may be grown for summer beet and also for storing. Long beets are not now in favour among gardeners. Beetroot is usually deep red in colour. Very new to Britain is 'Burpee's Golden' with orange red skin and yellow flesh.

Sowing Beet seedlings are noted for 'bolting' if seed is sown too early. The introduction of 'Boltardy' now permits seed to be sown as early as the first half of April. In the north of England cloches come in handy for this early sowing.

Other beets should not be sown until

Above: After the leaves have been twisted off, lay the beetroots on sand in a box and cover them with more sand

the second half of April or early May. Sowings of a quick maturing round beet may be sown again in late May and in June.

Sow seeds thinly in 1-in. deep seed drills spaced at 12 in. apart. If you sow under cloches leave only 8 in. between rows.

Hoe between rows to keep down weeds. If you have sown too thickly pull out some seedlings when the soil is wet. Do not thin seedlings too drastically. Pull young beets for summer salads in July just as soon as they are large enough to cook. Continue to pull roots as and when wanted in the kitchen.

Lift beet for storing during October. Twist off the foliage and rub off any dry soil adhering to the roots. Store, sandwich fashion, in dry ashes or peat. Apple and orange boxes are useful storage containers. It is important to house them in a cool but frost-free place.

Begonias

Large-flowered begonias are usually grown from tubers, but they can be grown from seed and they will flower about eight months after sowing if sufficient heat is available.

Growing from Seed Sow seed of tuberous double varieties and *B. semperflorens* in January or early February, in soilless compost of J.I. seed compost. Sow in a clay half pot or pan, and when using a soilless compost do not firm it down. Before sowing water the compost. Sprinkle the seed on the surface of the compost and do not cover it with additional compost, or with paper to exclude light. Place the pan in

Below: 'Rosanna', a double-flowered tuberous begonia

Above: Varieties of Begonia semperflorens

a heated propagator, and maintain a temperature of 60°–70°F (15°–21°C). The seed should germinate in 8–14 days and the seedlings should be pricked out as soon as possible, into a similar compost, about 1 in. apart. Return them to the propagator if possible and, after a further 4–6 weeks, the seedlings should be touching each other, and they will then need spacing 2 in. apart. Return to the propagator again for a

few weeks, but if this is not practicable, keep them as warm as possible and if it is dull or cool they will need very little water. By mid-May the seedlings should be hardened off in a frame prior to planting out in early June. They like some peat or similar material in the soil, and they can be planted in shade or full sun. Plants to be grown in pots in the greenhouse should be potted up into 3-in. pots in early May, in 1 part, by bulk, of J.I.P. 1 compost, mixed with 1 part of soilless compost.

Feeding Plants in Pots When in bloom tuberous double begonias will need a weekly feed with a weak tomato-type fertilizer, high in potash. Stop feeding in early September. Plants will need less water as the cooler weather arrives, but it is vital that the compost should be kept moist and no attempt should be made to force the plants into dormancy by withholding water. As top growth ceases slight moisture is needed at the roots to help build up a good tuber to survive the winter dormancy.

Winter Treatment Any green leaves retained by the end of October can then be removed, but the stems must not be forcibly pulled off. Stop watering as soon as all green leaves have dropped, or been removed, and the stems should drop off within a few days. The tubers can then be taken from the pots and cleaned up, but be careful not to damage the 'eyes' (axillary buds) on the top of the tuber as next year's growth will start from these. Store the tubers in dry peat in a frost-proof place until the following spring when they can be re-started. Plants in the garden should be lifted in early October with a ball of soil round the roots, placed on the floor of the greenhouse until all stems have dropped, then stored in dry peat.

'Judy Langdon', another popular double-flowered tuberous begonia

Bird Tables

There is no doubt that encouraging birds is one way of increasing the interest and fascination of a garden. There is a school of thought which says that birds do a lot of damage in the garden but the actual harm they do is relatively slight. A problem may arise if soft fruit is being grown but the modern garden cages or nets will reduce damage considerably.

One way of encouraging birds in the garden is to construct a bird table on which suitable bird food and scraps can be placed. It is always advisable to keep a bird table well above ground level so that cats cannot reach the birds as they feed.

A small bird table can be attached to a suitable tree but it is very important that the table is well away from branches which might give access for cats. Try if possible to place the bird table away from prevailing winds.

A simple design consists of a reasonably thick sheet of plywood which has had one side cut out to fit well round part of the tree trunk. The platform must be supported by a triangular piece of timber cut from 1-in. thick timber. This should support *most* of the platform across its width. The triangular section should be nailed to the trunk and the platform screwed to it. On suitable large trees, several of these small bird tables can be fastened to the trunks to provide interesting places to watch the birds from the house windows.

Sometimes a small old tree can be a problem. This can be used as a bird table with a large platform screwed to its top. Old tree branches can be sawn to length to provide unusual supports for bird table tops and if selected carefully, their graceful bends and twists will add considerably to their eye-appeal and general appearance.

Blackberries

The Care of Blackberries

Blackberries and the other berry fruits are all very easy to grow. They fruit on canes produced during the previous year. After planting, cut down to a sound bud about 9 in. above the ground. Shoots which grow during the first summer will fruit in the second year. After picking, cut old canes to ground level and tie the new season's canes against the horizontal support wires. It is sound practice either to spread out the old canes all to one side of the plant, tying the new ones in on the other side, or to spread out the fruiting canes on both sides, but fairly low down, and fasten the new canes to the centre and along the top. These schemes, by keeping the new canes separate from or above the old ones, are designed to prevent them from becoming disease infected by drip from above.

Blackcurrants

The Care of Blackcurrants

Plant slightly deeper than the bushes were in the nursery, put down a 2-in. mulch of rotted manure, compost or peat and at once cut all shoots down to within an inch of the mulch. The next winter cut down half of the new shoots; those which remain will give you your first crop. In subsequent years prune as soon as the crop has been picked, removing entirely about one third of the shoots which have just fruited. Blackcurrants yield most heavily on the young wood of the previous summer's growth but also on two-year-old and older wood. Try to keep the centre of the bush from becoming congested.

Feeding Blackcurrants are gross feeders. Liberal dressings (5 lb. per sq. yd.)

Above: Blackcurrant 'Baldwin'

Below: Pruning a blackcurrant bush by removing about one third of the stems that have fruited after cropping

in winter or early spring with rotted farm or stable manure are best. Also scatter $\frac{1}{3}$ oz. of sulphate of potash and 1 oz. of sulphate of ammonia per sq. yd. in spring. Every third year add 1 oz. of superphosphate per sq. yd. Where no natural dung is available mulch freely with garden compost, lawn mowings or peat, and double the sulphate of potash and treble the sulphate of ammonia dressings.

Bonsai Trees

Bonsai This is a technique, originating in China and Japan, for producing miniature replicas of mature trees by careful root and stem pruning and training. The most valuable bonsai are, however, originally collected as naturally gnarled and dwarfed specimens from exposed mountain sides which are further trained and improved.

Picea pungens 'Glauca' and 'Chestnut' or 'Buckeye' (*Aesculus*) are good for beginners. Each can be trained into a typical artificially dwarfed tree or 'bonsai'. The bonsai art is one that has been in being in Japan and China for centuries, spreading first to the U.S.A., and later to the U.K. Bonsai are charming and fascinating plants that are assets on a very temporary basis in interior decoration. For this purpose excellent specimens can be bought, but old ones are costly. Anybody can, however, dwarf trees by gathering their seeds and seedlings from the garden and by taking cuttings and planting them in a suitable potting compost.

After they have become well established, the dwarfing process can begin. The procedure is:

Transplant the plants into individual cream cartons with small holes punched in their sides and bottom, using a mild potting compost like J.I.P. 1.

Prune for two years any roots that appear through the apertures. During the second year, shape the plant by pinching out growing tips to encourage bushiness, shortening shoots and removing unwanted ones to make the outline of the dwarf conform to that of its giant counterpart.

At the beginning of the third year, after root pruning, plant the bonsai in poor soil (2 parts of the potting compost and 1 part coarse sand).

Left: The chestnut tree in dwarf form

Bottle Gardens

Bottle Gardens The use of closed glass containers for growing plants in the home. Large bottles such as carboys are ideal, though even smaller containers can house one or two plants. This method is ideal for growing the more delicate plants, particularly ferns, that require a humid, dust-free environment, though a wide range of house plants can be grown. Aquaria and terraria may also be used for the same purpose and are a near approach to the glazed boxes invented early in the nineteenth century by Dr. Nathaniel Ward. Known as Wardian cases, these containers were invaluable for transporting living plant material on long ocean voyages. Often in fancy shapes, they were a prominent feature in many Victorian houses.

Bottle gardens or jungle jars as they are sometimes called are extremely decorative and have great charm but apart from these qualities they can also play a useful role. In them it is possible to grow many plants which cannot be expected to do so well outside the glass walls, in rooms where the atmosphere is dry and the temperature sometimes fluctuates.

A bottle garden offers you the choice of adding to your collection of house plants. Some of the more choosy plants you can expect to grow – and can buy – are species of selaginella (Club mosses) which are mossy and fern-like and carpeting; *Nertera depressa*, another carpeting (but much more difficult) plant with tiny leaves and little orange berries; many kinds of the tender ferns such as the wiry-stemmed maidenhairs, miniature tender palms, crotons, fittonia, calathea, maranta, peperomia, pellacea, pilea and pellionia. Some of these you will recognize as being good room plants under certain conditions and the important thing about using these in bottle gardens is that most are fairly slow growing. They also provide colour and texture contrast. It is possible to fill a bottle with just one type of plant, say a colony of bromeliads or ferns, but usually they look more attractive when the plants are mixed.

Unless you know your plants well, do not be led into thinking that if a plant is small and has small leaves it is bound to be suitable for this type of garden. Helxine, now known botanically as *H. soleirolii*, sometimes called baby's tears, has the tiniest leaves yet it

Planting a bottle garden. Strew a few nuggets of charcoal on the floor of the container before adding sand for drainage. Slope the soil slightly. Put the lowest plant in first near the front, cover its roots with soil and put the next plant in position

would soon take over the entire bottle. The same applies to the creeping ficus (*F. rumila*), to tradescantia and zebrina. Of course, if you find that a plant is growing too rapidly you can always take it out and pot it in the usual manner and grow it elsewhere. If you have a bottle garden for several years, this becomes necessary.

Jungle jars have become so popular that today special glass containers are being produced for this purpose. Unlike the old-fashioned glass carboys these are made with necks large enough to allow an arm to reach down inside. Another and easy-to-fill jungle jar is an outsize brandy balloon type glass. Storage jars and even wine and cider jars and bottles can be used, so long as it is possible to plant them.

The glass is usually clear and is preferable to that tinted light brown, light blue or green which obscures much of the light. The important thing is that it should be clean and be kept clean.

If the neck of the glass is large enough for you to insert your hand, planting will offer few problems but when you are filling a jar which has a narrow neck you should be both careful and patient.

First group the plants in the way you hope to see them in the jar.

If you cannot insert your hand you will need to improvise a tool or two so that you can make a hole for the plant, guide the plant into the hole, cover it and firm the soil round the plant afterwards. Often one thick stick will do the lot but more often it is helpful to lash a kitchen spoon to a cane to dig out holes. An old-fashioned wooden cotton reel on the end of a cane will make a neat little rammer with which you will be able to pat the soil round the plants. These should always be set firmly in the soil otherwise their roots will not be able to absorb nourishment and they may sicken and die.

As with all containers, troughs, large bowls, dish gardens, a drainage layer is essential. The safest thing to put in is charcoal, which is so light in weight that it cannot crack the glass. If you use small pebbles such as pea gravel, do this with care, perhaps a thin layer of peat to cushion the impact of the stones on the glass base.

To fill a carboy, make a funnel or cylindrical chute of strong paper or card. Insert one end of this into the neck of the jar. First pour in the peat, then the gravel and lastly the soil.

This drainage layer needs to be quite deep, 2 in. or so for a large carboy and proportionately less for smaller jars.

Composts should not be too rich or the plants will grow too fast. The best medium is John Innes Potting Compost No. 2. The amount of soil you use will depend upon the size of the container; you should be able to see much more glass and plants than soil but it is the depth of the plants' roots which should guide you. These must be properly planted.

To get the soil in the right condition so far as moisture is concerned, calculate how much you need, take about one third of this amount and spread this out on newspaper to dry. Spray the other two thirds until it is just moist, uniformly so, and when you take a handful and squeeze it gently it should just cling together. This dampened compost should go in first. The dry compost follows to form a top dry layer which should help to seal in the moisture. As with dish gardens, water the plants beforehand and allow them to drain thoroughly. Knock them from their pots in turn. If the aperture of the glass is very small it may be necessary to shake off any loose soil from the roots so that the plant can be slipped in easily. The leafy portion is no problem because this naturally contracts as it is eased root first through the opening. To make sure of this, hold the plant by the tips of its leaves, or if it is tall, gather its branches or leaves up near its centre stem, so that this top portion is made really slim. Make a hole in the soil, tilt the jar and aim for the hole. This actually, is easier than it sounds. Direct the plant into the hole with the stick or with the spoon. Make the hole for the next plant directing the soil round the roots of the first plant. Settle the soil down before tilting the jar for the second time. Continue this way until all the plants are in position.

Inevitably, some soil particles will dirty the inside of the jar. It is not wise to spray these off with water, which seems the natural thing to do, because the soil will be made too wet. A feather duster fixed to a strong piece of wire, which can be bent as required, is the easiest way to clean the glass. If the plants' leaves have soil on them, lash a fine paint brush to a cane and clean them.

If the soil is properly moist the plants should settle in and you should not need to water it for some weeks. If the balance is right you should see a little condensation or dew on the interior each morning. However, if this seems excessive – so much that there are several runnels and large drops on the glass, there is too much moisture in the soil and it would be prudent to remove the moisture from the glass to prevent it running back into the soil. Lash a tissue to the end of a wire or the bow of a coat-hanger to do this. When the time comes that you see no condensation, this is an indication that the soil needs watering. To do this, gently spray the interior glass. This will help to clean it at the same time. Do not feed the soil or the plants will grow too well.

Broccoli
Calabrese

See 25 (Cabbage family) for recommended growing methods.

Calabrese This appears in catalogues as 'Green Sprouting Broccoli', 'Italian Sprouting Broccoli' or simply as 'Calabresse'. It is a winter/autumn vegetable. Sow in April and set out plants in June. A green central head will form on each plant in August or September. Cut and use this as cauliflower. Thick side shoots are then produced; these may be cooked as asparagus, after removing the leaves and peeling the stems.

Bulbs and Corms

See individual entries for popular favourites.

General Cultivation

Roughly speaking and if no special instructions are given the depth at which to plant a bulb is not more than twice its depth of soil above it and not less than its depth. Indoors, bulbs can be grown in pots filled with ordinary potting compost, in bowls or other undrained containers filled with a specially prepared bulb fibre, which is usually a fibrous of sphagnum peat with crushed shell and small pieces of charcoal, to prevent the fibre from becoming sour as a result of water collecting in the undrained bowl. The fibre has no food value, though the bulbs can be fed very carefully with a liquid feed. If grossly overwatered the roots in a bowl will rot. If you think a bowl has been overwatered tilt it very carefully, holding the fibre in with one spreadeagled hand and drain off such water as appears. Bulbs for the house should be started into growth in a cool dark place such as a cold cupboard or a plunge bed in the garden. This is merely a flat area on which the pots can be stood and covered completely with about 2 in. of moist peat, sand or washed ashes.

The planting depths for outside should not be followed inside. Large bulbs are usually planted with little or no compost over the last $\frac{1}{2}$–1 in. If the neck of the bulb is above the surface take care not to water into it. Plant the bulbs close, but not actually touching, and choose a bowl deep enough to contain all the roots which will otherwise come out at the surface, or through the drainage holes of too small a pot. Pack the compost down round the bulbs which may shrink and need top-dressing later on. Leave a space at the top to allow the application of water.

A very fine display of daffodils can be obtained by planting a double layer in a large, deep pot. Plant the lower layer about half way up the pot and cover all but the tips of the noses with compost, then stagger the top layer above them so that all the noses have a straight run to the surface. Cover the top bulbs as usual.

Left: Tulip 'Engadin'

Right: Crocus chrysanthus 'Cream Beauty'

Bulbs in the Greenhouse

These are planted in pots of one of the J.I.P. composts, often with sharp drainage below. Small bulbs should be covered with their own depth of soil and large ones may be only half submerged. Bulbs near the surface are more likely to need careful staking.

Watering

Many bulbs fail completely if they become dry at any time when they are growing, but only plants which are growing strongly need much water in winter as less is lost by evaporation than in summer, and such plants should be watered on the soil only. Water on the leaves may lead to fungal infection.

Ripening

This is the name given to the complex chemical processes which occur inside the bulbs both before and after the leaves die down. Potash appears to be essential for these changes, as are the gradual withdrawal of water and, in many but not all, baking by sun heat.

It is important that bulbs be ripened in the sun and not be smothered with other plants or weeds. Internal changes continue during the resting period and can be adversely affected by incorrect storage temperature.

Resting

When the leaves of a bulb start to turn yellow watering must stop and the bulb be rested, unless experience shows otherwise. Many can stand being dried right out; tulips like a thorough baking.

As far as many greenhouse pot plants

are concerned the bulbs or corms are best left in the soil in the pot until it is time to start them into growth again. This prevents them withering as much as they would do in the open air and keeps them relatively safe.

Bulbs in the garden should be left to finish their growth before lifting, cleaning and sorting. If they are not to be lifted it may be wise to mark the site.

Grass with bulbs in it must not be mown until the foliage turns yellow, nor should the foliage be picked with the flowers. The leaves make the stored food.

Bulbs in bedding schemes may need to be moved before it is time to rest them. They can be lined up in trenches to finish their growth.

Bulbs which have been forced for use in the house or for cutting should not be used again for this purpose the following year.

Starting into Growth
Bulbs still in pots can be put into fresh compost like new bulbs, or some of the old compost can be removed and replaced by fresh, or the whole pot ball can be transferred to a larger pot and top-dressed. It is usually, but not al-ways, necessary to water the soil to start growth. If a pot shows signs of growth it must be watered, but the amount given at first should be modest.
Suitable Sites There is some bulb, corm or tuber suitable for growing in almost any place you can name, though most prefer a sunny position. The following are some interesting possibilities:

(1) Display beds devoted to nothing else: hyacinths, greigii tulips, dahlias.
(2) To grow through other bedding plants: Darwin tulips through wallflowers or forget-me-nots, Cannas through summer bedding plants or annuals.
(3) To edge beds: Dutch crocuses, short alliums, muscari, zephyranthes, chionodoxa, scillas, puschkinia.
(4) In clumps (groups) in mixed borders. Tall alliums, crocosmia, daffodils, summer snowflakes, crown imperial, camassia, some lilies, galtonia, dahlias, tall tulips.
(5) In beds for cutting: gladioli, dahlias, narcissi, irises (Dutch, English and Spanish), St. Brigid and De Caen anemones, some alliums.
(6) Naturalized in long grass: narcissi (daffodils).
(7) Naturalized in short turf: tiny daffodils, fritillaries, muscari.
(8) Naturalized under deciduous shrubs or trees: *Anemone blanda*, eranthis, cyclamen, snowdrops, colchicums.
(9) Naturalized in thin woodland: some alliums, bluebells, erythroniums, ornithogalum, *Galanthus nivalis*.
(10) On rock gardens: choice fritillaries, small irises, small narcissi, crocus species, some alliums.
(11) Grown in alpine houses or cold frames: winter-flowering crocuses, small irises, cyclamen, *Anemone blanda*, small fritillaries, autumn snowflakes, small South African corms.
(12) Grown in hot borders under south-facing walls: ixias, nerine, amaryllis, pancratium, babiana, sternbergia, sparaxia, crinum.
(13) In warm but moist places: tigridia, ranunculus, chincherinchee.
(14) Grown in cool borders among evergreen shrubs: most lilies, galtonia, colchicums.
(15) Grown in pots or vases on a terrace: hyacinths, daffodils, begonias.
(16) Grown in pots or bowls indoors: hyacinths, daffodils, early tulips, crocuses, muscari, scillas, dwarf irises, hippeastrum, vallota.

Indoor bulbs 1: Place a good layer of moist bulb fibre in the pot 2: Place bulbs in position 3: Press more moist fibre around bulbs, leaving tips exposed 4: Put pot in polythene bag before plunging it under sand, ashes, etc.

Left: Narcissus Actaea

Cabbage Family
The Cabbage Tribe
Sow brassica seeds in a special bed of fertile soil, which, after it has been dug, should be raked level and firmed with the feet. Make 1-in. deep drills, 8 in. apart. If the soil is dry, fill the seed drills with water; allow the water to drain away before sowing fairly thickly. The seedlings will not remain in the bed for very long so that the ill effects of overcrowding will be minimal.

Varieties
Brussel Sprouts 'Indra' (F_1); 'Irish Elegance'; 'King Arthur' (F_1); 'Peer Gynt' (F_1); 'Prince Askold' (F_1).
Cabbage (Summer) 'Babyhead'; 'Grey-

Cabbage 'May Star'

hound'; 'May Star' (F_1); 'June Star' (F_1); 'Primo'.
Cabbage (Autumn) 'Autumn Monarch' (F_1); 'Autumn Pride' (F_1).
Cabbage (Winter) 'Christmas Drumhead'; 'January King'; 'Winter Monarch' (F_1).
Cabbage (Spring) 'April'; 'Harbinger'.
Cabbage (Savoy for Winter) 'Ormskirk Late Green'; 'Best Of All'.

Purple sprouting broccoli

Cauliflower (Spring) 'All the Year Round'; 'Arcturus'.
Cauliflower (Summer) 'All the Year Round'.
Cauliflower (Autumn) 'Boomerang'; 'Canberra'.
Cauliflower Broccoli 'Reading Giant'.
Sprouting Broccoli Calabresse, 'Green Comet' (F₁); Purple Sprouting Broccoli; White Sprouting Broccoli.
Kale 'Dwarf Green Curled'.

Weed and water when necessary. In a frame or beneath cloches you may have to water frequently. Remove the frame light and take off cloches in May.

Brassica plants do best in firm fertile soil. The evening before transplanting water the seed bed well if it is dry.

Make holes with a dibber. If the soil is dry fill the holes with water and allow it to soak away. Take seedlings out of the seed bed, choosing sturdy, straight specimens. Lower a plant into each hole until the lowest leaf is level with the surrounding soil. Push the dibber into the ground alongside, to press soil against the root and stem of the plant. Plant cauliflowers only to the depth at which the seedling was growing in the seed bed.

Cabbage root maggot is a fairly common pest. Eggs are laid alongside brassica plants often after they have been transplanted. The maggots bore into the roots. Plants are dwarfed or may wilt and usually die. The female flies find the plants by sense of smell. The scent from newly-planted brassica seedlings can be masked by setting out plants in firm ground mulched with garden compost.

Club root is a common and serious disease. Affected plants make poor growth and are often stunted; the roots are badly swollen and may smell nasty. Badly drained and acid soils favour the fungus. Regular heavy dressings of compost lower soil acidity and improve drainage. Dressing with lime also

Transplanting Dates and Distances

Vegetable	Date	Between rows (inches)	Between plants in the rows (inches)
Brussels sprouts	May/June	30	30
Cabbage – summer	May/June	15–18	15–18
autumn, winter	June		
spring	September/October		
Cauliflower – spring	Move plants to cold frame in October. Transplant to final positions in spring	18–24	18
summer, autumn	June		
Cauliflower broccoli (Winter cauliflower)	June	24–30	18–24
Sprouting broccoli	June/July	24–30	18–24
Kale (Borecole)	June/July	24–30	18–24

When to Sow

Vegetable	Cloche or cold frame	Outdoors
Brussels sprouts	March	early April
Cabbage – early summer	March	early April
late summer	—	mid April
autumn	—	mid April
winter	—	mid April
spring	—	late July/early August
Cauliflower – spring	—	August*
summer	—	early April
autumn	—	mid April/May
Cauliflower broccoli	—	mid April
Sprouting broccoli	—	mid April
Kale	—	mid April

*Overwinter plants in cold frame or cloches.

Cabbage 'June Star'

26

Above: Cabbage 'Blood Red'

counteracts acidity.

Hoe and water often; plants weakened by drought are particularly prone to attack by caterpillars of the cabbage moth and cabbage white butterflies. Strong, healthy brassica plants may be visited by cabbage white butterflies and by the cabbage moth. They are rarely a nuisance to plants making good, steady growth. If you spot any small caterpillars, pick them off. Spray with a weak solution of table salt and water. The best preventive measure is to ensure that the soil is fertile and that plants are never short of water in summer.

Start picking Brussels sprouts near the base of the stem in late autumn/early winter. Continue harvesting until the top of the stem is reached. Cut tops of the plant in February and March for use as 'Spring greens'.

Harvest cabbages when they are firm and tight. Cut cauliflowers and cauliflower broccoli when heads are well formed and snowy white.

Pick side shoots of sprouting broccoli in winter and spring. Finally cut and use the central head, a loose collection of shoots. Cut the central, loose heads of kale for use in late winter or early spring. Side shoots will develop; pick these when they are still young.

Red Cabbage   This is often grown for pickling. Sow seeds in August and give the seedlings cloche protection until they are planted out at 18 in. apart each way in late March/early April. Seeds may also be sown in early spring and seedlings transplanted in June.

Cacti

The cactus family is native to America; plants seen in Europe and elsewhere have been introduced at some time in the past. There are three distinct types of plant, the pereskias, the epiphytes and the desert cacti, and these require different treatment because of their differing 'home' conditions. Except for the pereskias, they are stem succulents, having either no leaves or small temporary ones. Cacti are not all spiny plants, some being strongly armed while others are quite spineless. All cacti have areoles, small pincushion-like structures scattered over the stems. Spines (when present), off-shoots, and branches come from these areoles. This is the way to distinguish a cactus from another stem succulent, such as a euphorbia, which does not have areoles. Also all cactus flowers have the same general design, while those of other succulents differ enormously between the various families.

Pereskias   The pereskias must have a brief mention here, as they are a very

Below: Opuntia microdasys

small group of primitive cacti. Most growers regard them as curiosities, and they are not very common in collections.

Epiphytic Cacti   By contrast, the epiphytes are commonly grown in this country, many being sold as florists' plants. Although there is no shortage of water where the plants are found, the pockets of humus they grow in dry out very quickly. Epiphytic cacti have no leaves, but flattened, slightly succulent stems, sometimes incorrectly called 'leaves'. These stems may consist of short segments, as in the familiar 'Christmas cactus' (schlumbergera), the flowers appearing on the ends of the segments, or the stems may be long and strap-like, as in the epiphyllums.

They need a good, porous soil; J.I.P.2 with some additional leafmould or peat and grit is suitable. Leafmould is ideal if it can be obtained as it more closely resembles the natural soil of the forests. The soilless composts are also very suitable for these and other cacti, but for the epiphytes, the lime-free type of compost is best. It helps to add a teaspoon of bonemeal to each pot of compost. Re-potting should be done annually. These cacti will survive winter temperatures as low as 41°F (5°C), but flower much better if kept a little warmer. They should be kept moist all the year round. In fact, it is best to forget that they are cacti and treat them as normal pot plants. When in bud, epiphytes can be fed once a fortnight with a tomato-type potassium fertilizer.

Because these epiphytic cacti grow among trees, they do not need full sunlight. They make very successful house plants if grown on an east-facing window-ledge, where they will receive the early morning sun, but are in shade during the heat of the day. They grow rapidly, and when a plant outgrows a 6-in. pot, it should be replaced by cuttings. A stem is cut from an epiphyllum, or a few segments from the schlumbergeras and rhipsalidopsis. The cutting is allowed to dry for two or three days, and then potted up. This drying period for cactus and other succulent cuttings is always carried out to prevent rot from spreading into the fleshy stems. They do not wilt during this period as other plants would. The best time of the year for taking cuttings is April–May, although it is quite possible at any time during spring and summer.

Desert Cacti The desert cacti are the spiny tall or round plants that we associate with the American deserts. Many are found growing on rocky mountain sides and in grassy areas, as well as in the sandy regions of Mexico and South America. They all need the maximum amount of sunlight to flourish and flower freely. For this reason they do not make such good house plants as the epiphytes. If a greenhouse is not available, they should be kept on a south-facing window-sill, and preferably stood outdoors from May to September.

A minimum winter temperature of 41°F (5°C) is adequate for most desert cacti. A well-drained compost is essential. If about a third extra grit or sharp sand is added to J.I.P.2, this will make a suitable compost. Alternatively, a soilless compost may be used. Since the food content of the soil does not last forever, the plants should be repotted annually.

Many people seem to think that cacti need no water! This is far from the truth, although they will certainly survive a period of dryness (after all they are adapted to do just this). This means

Above: The flowering cactus Rebutia calliantha krainziana

Right: The Christmas cactus, Schlumbergera 'Buckleyi'

that it is not necessary to worry too much while you are on holiday (although seedlings will suffer). But without water they will just survive, not grow, and the plants should be kept more or less continually moist between April and October. The watering should be reduced after this and they should be left dry during December and January, if kept in a greenhouse. Watering can be restarted gradually as the light improves in February. If the plants are wintered in a heated house with a very dry atmosphere, more water will be needed during winter to prevent excessive shrivelling. Indoors, the ideal winter spot is an unheated room, but this may not always be possible. The reason for keeping them dry at this time is that if they grow in the poor light of winter, they are likely to become distorted and may rot the next year. Also, flowering is dependant on the previous winter's treatment.

compost heap or in a hole in the ground.

Dig carrots on a dry day in October. Cut back the foliage to 1 in. from the crown of each carrot. Store carrots in a pit or in boxes sandwich-fashion between damp sand. Keep boxes in a cool place such as an outhouse, shed or garage.

Cauliflowers

Cauliflowers are greedy plants. Do not order cauliflower seeds unless you know your soil is very fertile. Planting cauliflowers in poor soil is a waste of time and garden space. See Cabbage for 'How to Grow'.

Celeriac or Turnip-Rooted Celery

Sow seeds in heat in March or April, harden off the plants and plant them 1 ft. apart in the garden in May. Remove all suckers. Lift and store the roots in October. Store as carrots.

Celery

There are three sorts – blanched, self-blanching and green. Sow seeds in trays or pots in a heated greenhouse in March. Harden off plants in a cold frame before planting outdoors in early June. Those which need blanching are

Celery 'Giant Red'

set out in a trench; earth up plants slightly in mid-August, continue the operation two weeks later and finish it a fortnight afterwards. Start digging blanched celery in November. A good place for self-blanching celery is a cold frame. Plant 9 in. apart. Remove the frame light in late June and in mid-July tuck straw around the plants to assist blanching. Lift plants for use in August and September. Green (American Green) celery is grown in the same way as self-blanching celery but because it is eaten green there is no blanching to be done at all and plants may be grown in the open.

Cherries

The Care of Cherries
Sweet cherries are not grown much in gardens because there are no dwarfing rootstocks yet available and because, as none is self-fertile, you must have two trees. Fan-trained trees are a possibility but even root-pruning will probably be necessary to restrain vigour.

The Morello sour cherry is a different proposition because it is self-fertile and less vigorous. It can be grown as a bush or be fan-trained and as most fruit is

Morello cherries

borne on the previous year's growth pruning (in spring after the buds have broken) should be directed towards stimulating new growths, as with peaches, old fruited shoots being cut out and a few complete old branches being taken out each year from established trees.

Cherries flourish best in deep medium loam as typified by the brick-earth soil found in Kent. They also prosper on a deep heavy loam, but will not tolerate poor drainage and soon show manganese deficiency on a chalky soil.

Chicory

Sow seeds 1 in. deep in early June and thin seedlings to 9 in. apart. In November dig up the parsnip-like roots and heel them in a trench over which a little straw should be spread. Take small batches for chicon production now and then during the winter. Trim roots back by a few inches and reduce the foliage to within 1 in. of the crown. Plant roots closely in the greenhouse border and cover with straw weighed down with dry soil. Inspect for chicons after a month or so. Alternatively, plant prepared roots in pails or pots and force chicons indoors or in a garage or shed. It is important that all light be excluded.

Chrysanthemum

Strictly, this genus includes pyrethrums and also marguerites or Shasta daisies. The white-flowered *C. maximum* 'Esther Read' is the best known, but excellent varieties include 'Thomas Killin', 'Everest', large single white flowers; 'Wirral Supreme', double white, very large lacy-petalled single flowers; 'Cobham Gold', 'Moonlight' both flushed with yellow; 'Esther Read' and 'Jennifer Read', all doubles. But as a garden plant *C. corymbosum* is preferable. This has greyish foliage, grows stoutly to $3\frac{1}{2}$ ft. and bears hundreds of 1-in. wide white daisies from June to August. Even after Michaelmas daisies are over *C. uliginosum*, 5–6 ft., comes into flower; it has single white, yellow-centred daisies 2 in. across which add a last touch of summer to late autumn.

There are many gay varieties of annual chrysanthemums, single and double. All have daisy-like flowers on good stems and often have rings or zones of colour on white or cream petals. Among the best hardy annuals for summer flowering, they make excellent cut flowers. Seed should be sown in April in the open in a sunny position where they are to flower or in September for an early display the next year. They do not transplant readily, so it is a waste of time to plant out thinnings. They are not fussy about soil provided it is not excessively wet.

Obtaining Plants The new grower should obtain his stock from a specialist nursery. In subsequent seasons it is possible to raise new stock from the stools of the previous year. A stool is what is left when the flowers have been cut and the main stem is shortened to about 12 in.

Propagation Though in many areas the chrysanthemum is hardy, it is better to take up the stools, wash them free of soil and then box them up in fresh compost. J.I.P.1 will do very well. Keep the soil fairly dry throughout the winter and house the stools in a cold greenhouse or cold frame. In early spring the stool will send up young shoots; once growth has begun give sufficient water to keep the soil moist. Growth can be hastened by applying gentle bottom heat but temperature should not rise far above 50°F (10°C). Propagation may now proceed by either of two methods. If the shoots have roots already developed they may be taken off and boxed up to make new plants. For various reasons, better plants are obtained by taking cuttings.

Clean, healthy young shoots some 2 in. long should be cut or broken off and inserted 1 in. deep in a box or bed of J.I.P.1. A thorough watering is then given and the container placed in a simple frame covered with butter muslin to shade the shoots from bright sunlight and to keep the air around them humid. This simple propagator may be placed either on the greenhouse bench or inside a cold frame. Since the optimum temperature for rooting is around 55°F (13°C) some slight warmth particularly in the form of bottom heat, will help matters greatly. If rooting hormones are used, well-rooted plants should be produced in a month.

Most early-flowering varieties root easily in March and April but those which bloom later in the greenhouse require a start in January and February.

Growing On The young plants must be gradually prepared to face the outside conditions. Earlies are grown either in boxes or in a bed of soil on the floor of the cold frame. Whichever method is used, they should be given plenty of room to develop and nothing less than 4-in. spacing will do. Since late-flowering plants are usually flowered in pots it is as well to start them in 3-in. pots, either clay or plastic, in J.I.P.1 or a soilless compost. As the pots fill with roots

it will be necessary to move the plants to 5- or 6-in. pots. J.I.P.2 will now be needed though, again, the soilless type will serve. A final potting will be needed later on into 8- or 9-in. pots using J.I.P.3. Make the compost little more than finger-firm so as to encourage rapid root extension. Late varieties can also be grown in the open garden and the plants lifted and replanted in the greenhouse in late September for flowering; the plants should be treated exactly as advised for the early-flowering varieties.

While plants are in the frame, guard against over-watering, frost and draughts. Gradually increase ventilation so that plants are hardened off by late April.

Soil Preparation Ideally the soil should be well drained yet retentive of moisture; fertile without being over-rich and open to all the light and air available. A liberal dressing of manure or other humus-forming material should be dug in during the winter and the surface left rough. About mid-April a dressing of 4 oz. per sq. yd. of a balanced fertilizer should be forked in to a depth of a few inches only, leaving the main body of the soil undisturbed.

The corn marigold

Raking to produce a good tilth is best left until a day or two before planting in May, the actual date depending on the prevailing weather conditions.

Planting The canes should first be inserted and the plants placed close to them, each one secured by a loose tie and protected from slug damage by the application of bait.

Late-flowering plants in pots are moved out to their summer quarters at the same time. Insert a cane in each pot and set out the pots in lines, securing the canes to a wire stretched about 4 ft. above the ground. Leave at least 1 ft. between the pots and 2 ft. between rows to allow free access.

Bud Development To obtain the best results it is helpful to understand the way in which a chrysanthemum plant develops. It begins with a single stem which extends until a flower bud appears in the growing point. This normally happens so early in the season that that the bud fails to develop into a flower but forces the plant to break into lateral growth thus forming a bushy habit. This bud is known as the *break bud*. In their turn, the laterals extend and in due time form buds. According to the time of year, either a cluster of buds or one bud surrounded by leafy shoots will be produced. Such buds are known as *first crown buds*. Where leafy shoots are produced around this bud, they will grow on strongly and produce further buds known as *second crown buds* and if the grower does not intervene the result is a large first crown flower struggling into bloom at the base of a cluster of much smaller flowers.

It is best to ignore the break bud since it is usual to remove the growing point of the young plant before that bud appears and the resultant branching is just the same. Early-flowering types are usually flowered on first crowns so merely pinch out the growing point when the plant is well established in the garden (about June 1st). When lateral growths are a few inches long remove the strongest and weakest, aiming to leave four to six of equal strength. When the first crown buds appear remove the growths surrounding the central bud on each shoot and allow them to flower. Some late-flowering types give better blooms on second crowns and the procedure is as follows. Two dates are given in the catalogue of varieties, which indicate

(a) when the plant is to be pinched first, and (b) when the laterals arising from that first pinch are to be stopped again by the removal of the growing points. The result will be a further crop of side shoots which are allowed to produce their buds to be dealt with as before by the removal of all buds except the central one. Two pinches will give far more stems than one but resist the temptation to flower them all. To obtain flowers of good size and quality the limit should be set at six to eight.

Sprays and pompon types are exceptions. These branch naturally, and all you need to do is to encourage the development of laterals by one pinch only, when the plants are 9–12 in. high. Since the beauty of these plants is in the large number of small starry blooms carried in sprays, no disbudding need be done. Nevertheless it may be wise to restrict the number of stems to ensure larger flowers.

Feeding By late May all plants will be growing away nicely in pots or the open garden and within some seven weeks the earlies will have to develop into mature bushes of up to eight stems each bearing its flower bud. Well-prepared, fertile ground will give fair results without further help but it is usually beneficial to give some added feed, firstly at the beginning of June to encourage quick establishment; secondly at the end of June to ensure that the plants are in vigorous health at the time the flower buds are being formed. Each time an application of a chrysanthemum fertilizer, in powder or liquid form, is all that is required.

Because late-flowering plants are usually grown in pots, feeding is more important. Liquid feeds are by far the best. It doesn't really matter what the label says so long as the relationship

Well-grown, early-flowering chrysanthemums

between the nitrogen and potash content is correct for the particular purpose. During the rapid development of leaf and stem there should be roughly twice as much nitrogen as potash. As the buds appear and are being dealt with, give only clear water but start feeding again when the buds have begun to swell, but now the nitrogen and potash contents must be roughly the same. Do not give heavy doses every ten days or so but give about a quarter the recommended strength every time you water.

Watering Correct use of the watering can is crucial to good growing but it is something which has to be learned rather than taught. With pots the safest rule is to apply water just before the plant threatens to wilt. Both the leaves and the soil surface will give clear indication when that point has been reached and enough water should be applied to moisten thoroughly the whole soil ball.

After Care Throughout the period of rapid growth it is necessary to train the plants. Remove surplus branches and shoots as soon as they are seen; tie flowering stems loosely to the cane every 9 in. or so. Never tie too tightly but, to avoid breakages, allow branches to sway a little in the breeze. Watch out for and deal with early pest infestations; the best insurance against pest damage is to keep the garden free of weeds.

Housing Plants Late-flowering types are flowered under glass. In late September, when the buds are beginning to show the first signs of colour, it is time to house the plants. Remove all old leaves to about one third of the height from the pot, remove all surplus growths; tie up the plants securely and place extra canes if necessary. Spray with an insecticide and with a systemic fungicide to combat mildews.

The greenhouse must be thoroughly

several days but it is good practice to give a little water say every two days rather than to wait until a pot is bone dry. In this latter condition the water will run all over the floor and cause damp air – the worst enemy of flowers indoors. After this the ventilators should be used in conjunction with the heating apparatus to maintain a dry moving atmosphere at a steady temperature of around 50°F (10°C). Light shading may be helpful in bright weather.

Flowering Time This is not only the season of satisfaction and enjoyment, it also provides opportunity for planning future efforts. Look critically at the plants and their flowers with a view to choosing those which have exhibited both vigour and excellence. These should be clearly marked so that they can be retained for the propagation of new stock. In this way the collection can be kept at a high level of health. There is much to be gained by visiting the local shows so as to see what is new and to chat with fellow enthusiasts.

Cutting Blooms Chrysanthemum blooms will last longer if they are cut

in the morning when the stems are full of sap. Place each stem in water immediately. Back at the house, bruise the lowest few inches of stem and remove all the leaves except three or four beneath the bloom. Now set the stems in a deep container of water and place it in a dark, cool place such as a garage or outhouse, for about 24 hours. After this treatment the flowers will last for several weeks, particularly if any stems which are further shortened are again bruised at the base.

Outdoor plants need not be cut right down at flowering time; in a mild autumn, it is not unusual to have a second crop of delightful sprays. Blooms may be small but the enriched colour and profusion of the flowers will more than compensate for lack of size.

Neither early nor late-flowering types should be cut right down after flowering. It is better to allow the sap to run back for a few weeks before shortening the main stem to about 12–18 in. In this state the stools can be boxed as described earlier. A final shortening to a few inches can be carried out in the spring.

Above: 'Golden Seal', a late-flowering variety

Right: 'Hagley Hybrid', a clematis; hard prune in January or February

cleaned. Remove all debris and any growing plants before burning a sulphur candle. When the fumes have dispersed, wash the glass and every crevice with a jet of water from the hosepipe. Test the heating apparatus and seal every leak in the roof.

Ideally there should be plenty of space around the plants inside but in practice one tends to pack them in rather tightly. In fact, it is far better to leave a few poor prospects outside so as to give the better plants more light and air. For the first ten days or so, leave doors and ventilators fully open. Watering will rarely be required for

Clematis

Clematis are some of the most beautiful climbing plants obtainable. They provide height and with their large and vivid flowers add splashes of colour over a long period. Given long canes or a background framework they will attach themselves and require no tying to their supports. Good size tubs are best, affording an extensive and cool root run. Some shade for the roots must be given and this is best done, either by planting some dense but shallow-rooting plants in the tub, or by placing tiles (or a collection of attractive pebbles from the beach) over their feet. The top growth, however, loves the sun. The most suitable for containers are those deciduous types which flower on the extremities of new growth as this allows for them to be pruned almost to the ground each year. With young plants this pruning is best done in February. *C. jackmanii* (deep-purple) and the many other named sorts offer a very wide choice of colour, from May to September. Propagate by stem cuttings in July.

A 'battlemented' yew hedge at Knightshayes Court, Devon

Coleus

(Half-hardy Perennial) 3 ft.
These are ornamental foliage plants with attractive leaves in shades of green, copper, red and apricot, making them conspicuous for greenhouse or room decoration. Sow seed of *C. blumei* or named hybrids in February under glass in a temperature of 75°F (24°C) (or as high a temperature as possible) and grow on without a check to obtain strong, showy plants. Particularly striking varieties may be perpetuated by taking cuttings, 3 in. long, of non-flowering shoots in August or March.

Some Popular Conifers

Evergreen Conifers
Chamaecyparis *C. lawsoniana*. The well-known Lawson's cypress is often recommended for evergreen hedges or taller screens, but is not ideal. Young seedlings must be used, as larger plants may at first be rocked by wind. It does not like very rich ground. Plant about 4½ ft. apart.

Cupressus

The Leyland cypress, *C. × leylandii*, is a splendid, hardy and adaptable tree. It is often recommended for hedges, but its rate of growth is so rapid that it will need cutting twice or more in a year, the last time in autumn. It is ideally suited for screens and windbreaks. Set the plants out 4–5 ft. apart.

The Monterey cypress, *C. macrocarpa*, has often been planted for hedges in the mildest districts. On all soils it is good. But even so, a particularly hard winter will kill isolated plants in a well established hedge, so destroying its appearance.

Thuya
T. plicata, the western red cedar in its native habitat, is a large western American forest tree. However, it stands clipping extremely well and is a hedge plant of great merit with glossy-green fragrant leaves in fern-like sprays. Plants should be set out at about 4½ ft. apart.

Cosmos

Cosmea (Half-hardy Annual) 2–3 ft.
This is a most decorative plant with fern-like foliage and large, single or semi-double, daisy-form flowers on slender but wiry stems which make it useful for cutting from July to October. The colour range includes orange, yellow, deep rose to brilliant vermilion, red and white. Sow the seed under glass in February and March in a temperature of 60°F (16°C). Prick out the seedlings and plant out in May in light, well-drained soil and in full sun.

Crocus

Iris Family
The large-flowered Dutch hybrids flower in March, and the little species crocus, by careful planning, will give flowers from September to March. The autumn and winter flowering ones are available from July to August and need to be put in immediately, as some will flower almost at once. The rest can be planted at any time during the autumn. The Dutch varieties are fine for edging beds and naturalizing in grass and the tiny ones are for alpine house or rock garden or, in many instances for planting under deciduous shrubs, or even for naturalizing in short grass (try *C. zonatus*, *C. speciosus*, *C. aureus* and *C. tomasinianus* for this). Plant the corms with not above 1 in. of soil over them. The flowers of the autumn flowering ones will come up before the leaves. Do not cut grass with crocus naturalized in it until the leaves have died

Right: Crocus tomasinianus

down. The corms like to be well sun baked during the summer. All may be grown in pans, the Dutch ones in bulb fibre also, but must not be brought into a warm place until the flowers are nearly out.

Dutch Varieties * = good forcer.
*Yellow Giant, early; *Vanguard, lilac, early; *Jeanne d'Arc, Kathleen Parlow, white; King of the Striped, lilac on white; Pickwick, lilac on purple; Queen of the Blues, lavender; Paulus Potter, reddish purple; *Purpurea grandiflora, violet.

Autumn and Winter Flowering Species
Zonatus, September, pale lilac, good naturalizer; *leucopharynx*, September, lavender with white throat; *speciosus*, September–October, blue, veined violet, all are good naturalizers; *albus*, white; Artabir, lavender; *aitchisonii*, china blue, pointed petals; Oxonian, deeper blue; Cassiope, October, blue; *cancellatus cilicicus*, September, lilac with purple veins; *sativus cashmeriana*, September–October, rosy lilac, the saffron crocus; *longiflorus*, October–November, lilac, striped purple, must have sunny spot, scented; *medius*, October–November, lilac-purple; *ochroleucus*, November–December, cream with orange base; *laevigatus fontenayi*, December–January, violet-blue.

Spring Flowering Species
Imperati, January–February, lilac, striped buff outside, good naturalizer; *ancyrensis*, orange-yellow, January–February, many flowers per corm, good indoors; *sieberi* Hubert Edelsten, January–February, vigorous, bluish-violet with yellow throat and white shading; *aureus*, January–February, yellow, spreads well by seed; *chrysanthus*, this has many named varieties, mostly excellent in pans; Blue Bird, purple and white; Blue Pearl, silvered blue; Cream Beauty, short, cream; E. A. Bowles, yellow, striped bronze; Ladykiller, purple and white; Snowbunting, lilac and white; Zwanenburg Bronze, deep yellow bronze outside; *tomasinianus*, January–February, variable shades of lavender, good naturalizer, seeds freely. Whitewell Purple is a dark selection; *balansae*, February–March, orange-yellow, pans; *biflorus weldenii*, February–March, white or blue and white; *etruscus* Zwanenburg, February–March, lavender blue, pans; *susianus* (Cloth of Gold), February–March, orange, striped bronze, pans, beds.

Cucumber

Cucumbers grown in the greenhouse or frame are tender plants. For the greenhouse you have a choice of varieties which bear male and female flowers or of all-female flowerers. For outdoors there are ridge kinds which roam over the ground and there are trellis cucumbers which need supports. There are varieties which bear both male and female flowers and new, all-female flowering kinds. Older, ridge sorts bear short cucumbers and the plants roam over the ground. Some newer varieties need a trellis to which plants may be tied; these are very suited to unheated greenhouses in the midlands and north.

Cucumber Varieties
(1) *Suitable for heated and unheated greenhouses* (F) = all-female flowerer 'Butcher's Disease-resisting'; 'Conqueror'; 'Femina' (F_1) (F); 'Feminex' (F_1) (F); 'Femspot' (F_1) (F); 'Improved Telegraph'; 'Rocket' (F_1); 'Topnotch' (F_1).
(2) *Suitable for the unheated frame in warmer areas* 'Conqueror'; 'Improved Telegraph'.
(3) *Suitable for the unheated frame or for outdoors – ridge sorts* 'Appleshaped'; 'Burpee Hybrid' (F_1); 'Burpless' (F_1); 'Greenline'; 'Long Green';

'Nadir' (F_1).
(4) *Suitable for the unheated greenhouse in most parts and for the open garden in the south – trellis sorts* 'Barton Vert' (F_1); 'Chinese Long Improved'; 'Kaga'; 'Kariha'; 'Ochiai Long Day' (F_1).
Sowing For greenhouse cultivation sow in late March. Otherwise, wait until late April. A temperature of 75°F (24°C) is needed for rapid germination. Sow two seeds in a $3\frac{1}{2}$-in. pot. Later pinch off the weaker seedling.

The border soil must drain well and should be rich in organic matter. A framework of wires or of canes and wires is needed, to which plants may be tied. Set out plants 2 ft. apart and do not plant deeply. Stop the plants when they reach the top of the supports. Prevent fruits from setting on the main stems by pinching off flower buds. Tie side shoots to horizontal wires and prune back these shoots to the second leaf beyond the first small cucumber on each of them. Cucumber plants like a warm, moist atmosphere, so keep plants well watered and spray with tepid water each evening in hot, sunny weather. In late July mulch the bed with a 1-in. layer of garden compost or strawy horse manure.

Frame Cultivation When plants have made four true leaves pinch out the growing point. As side shoots develop pinch these out too, at four leaves. Stop all fruit-bearing shoots at one leaf beyond each swelling cucumber and stop main lateral shoots when they reach the sides of the frame.

Ridge Cucumbers

Plant these in early June, 18 in. apart. When plants have made seven leaves nip out the central growing point to induce branching.

Trellis Cucumbers

Plant 1 ft. apart alongside a trellis 4–6 ft. high; a wire mesh garden fence or bean netting is suitable. Pinch out growing points of plants when they reach the top of the supports. Water often in dry weather.

Cyclamen
Primula Family

The tubers of cyclamen get bigger each year but do not make other small tubers, which are only obtained from seedling plants, the sole method of increase. The large greenhouse cyclamen obtainable around Christmas have

Cyclamen neapolitanum

been raised from seed. Unlike most of the small 'hardy' cyclamen the best display is from the new plant raised from seed after about 16 months in a warm greenhouse.

Species cyclamen are sold either in leaf or as dry corms; the latter should be treated with great care as the loss of the dormant buds sets the plants back permanently. Corms should be lightly covered with sieved leafmould or peat with some sharp sand and bonemeal, and should not have this pressed down. Similar compost should be used as a top-dressing every autumn.

All cyclamen have the characteristic swept-back petals, many have a colour range from white through pink to carmine, often with throat markings of carmine on the pale flowers, and many have beautiful marbling on their leaves.

The hardy cyclamen are invaluable tuberous-rooted plants for cool positions in the rock garden. Of the many cultivated species the three described are of outstanding virtue. They love lime but do not demand it. Plant them as growing tubers, not stored and dried ones which take a long time to grow. Plant 3–4 in. deep in soil rich in humus. Propagate by seeds. *C. europaeum* has marbled rounded leaves and pink fragrant flowers in summer; *C. neapolitanum* has beautifully shaped and marked leaves and deep pink – sometimes white – flowers in the autumn; *C. repandum* bears long-petalled rose-pink flowers in early spring. The dark green leaves are marbled with white.

The following can be grown outdoors August–September flowering: *C. europeaum*, fragrant with round leaves; *C. neapolitanum*, very hardy, marbled leaves. September flowering: *C. graecum*, velvety leaves. October–November flowering: *C. cilicium*, young leaves red beneath, marbled on top. December–March: *C. coum* (including *atkinsii*, *hiemale*, *ibericum*, *orbiculatum* and *vernum*), hardy and very variable, flowers small on short stalks. February–March: *C. creticum*, must be in shade, white flowered, fragrant, leaves red beneath. April–May: *C. repandum*, requires deep planting in sheltered woodland.

Cool house kinds *C. cyprium*, October flowering, fragrant, as are *C. balearicum* and *C. pseudibericum*, February–March flowering and *C. persicum*, March–April flowering; *C. libanoticum*, one of the loveliest, needs an alpine house.

Daffodil
Narcissus (Amaryllis family)

In gardens the narcissi are best divided into the large hybrids – for use naturalized in long grass, in beds for cutting and display, and in pots outdoors and in – and the small species and their hybrids – for use in short turf, on rock gardens, in pans in the alpine house or indoors. The official classification is based on flower colour and form, the relative length of the petal-like central ring or corona (which may be a trumpet, cup or eye) being of importance. The term daffodil is often restricted to the large trumpet forms, the others being called narcissi.

The bulbs of the small species are tiny; those of the garden hybrids are large and sold graded according to the number of 'noses' (growing points). Plant single-nosed bulbs with a bulb planter as there is no danger of them sticking half-way down the holes. The double and triple-nosed bulbs are fine for planting in borders or in pots where a close display of flowers is wanted.

Grass planted with daffodils must not be cut until the foliage has yellowed, nor should leaves be picked with flowers, for the foliage builds up the bulb with next year's flowers. If the grass is treated with normal lawn fertilizers there is no need to feed the bulbs (other than with bonemeal at planting), but bulbs in short turf must not receive lawn fertilizers as this will encourage the growth of coarse grasses.

Daffodils should be planted as soon as available, before hyacinths and tulips. Large bulbs require holes 6 in. deep and small ones 3–4 in. Bulbs in pots can be placed shoulder to shoulder with the noses just under or just above the surface. If intended for forcing they must be plunged in a cool moist place (with the exception of the variety Paper White) until the roots have developed well.

Dahlia

(Half-hardy Perennials) $1\frac{1}{2}$–2 ft.
Bedding varieties of dahlias are often treated as annuals as they are readily raised from seed. Dahlias require ample moisture during the growing season. Any outstanding plants should be lifted in the autumn after the first frost, and after the tubers have been washed and dried they should be stored in a frost-free place for the winter. They may be planted out the following spring and will start to flower in July. Or they can be put in a warm greenhouse in April to produce cuttings.

Dahlias are originally from Mexico, introduced into the British Isles about 1789. Very adaptable, they grow well in any type of soil. They are versatile, being used for garden decoration, cut flowers, floral art and exhibition. Few flowers can match them for their wide range of brilliant colours, their wide variety of shapes and sizes, and their

long flowering period. They tolerate extremes of climate and, even in a poor season, some kinds will produce over one hundred flowers.

Classification In height dahlias range from the Lilliput type, 1 ft. high, to the more normal types which can reach a height of over 5 ft., although the average is about $3\frac{1}{2}$ ft. The sizes of the blooms vary tremendously, from about 1 in. across to over 14 in. There are ten groups as follows:

Above: Collerette dahlia 'Nonsense'

Left: 'Pink Joy' a medium decorative type

DECORATIVE Fully double, the petals are broad and usually flat with rounded tips.
CACTUS Narrow petals rolled or quilled backwards half their length or more, sometimes curving inwards, sharply pointed.
SEMI-CACTUS Halfway between the previous two, the petals broad at the base and rolled for less than half their length.
(These three groups are divided into bloom sizes as follows: Giant, over 10 in.; large, 8–10 in.; medium 6–8 in.; small, 4–6 in.; miniature, not exceeding 4 in.)
BALL AND MINIATURE BALL These have a tight honeycomb formation

40

with short petals rolling inwards for half their length or more and rounded at the tips. Ball dahlias range from 4–6 in., miniature ball dahlias are 4 in. or less.

POMPON Smaller, more perfect than the ball dahlias and 2 in. or less in size.

SINGLE-FLOWERED A single row of petals surround an open centre.

ANEMONE-FLOWERED In these the flowers have numerous tubular petals surrounded by a single row of flat petals.

COLLERETTES These have a single inner row of small petals, usually of a different colour from the larger outer row of petals.

PEONY-FLOWERED These resemble the singles with an open centre but have two or more rows of petals.

MISCELLANEOUS In this group are those bizarre dahlias which as far as shape is concerned cannot be put in any of the other groups.

DWARF BEDDING DAHLIAS These belong to any of the ten groups but must not exceed 24 in. in height.

Site Dahlias prefer an open sunny position but will still grow well in a partially shaded spot, away from trees. They look glorious when massed in a bed or border by themselves. They also fit in well with other plants in the herbaceous border, if they are placed carefully to use their various heights and colours to best effect. The 1-ft. tall dwarf kinds will add summer colour to the rock garden, or can be planted in a bed in a retaining wall or even in a window box. Planted in tubs or other containers, they will brighten up a patio, terrace or other paved area.

Soil Cultivation Single digging is all that is necessary. This should be done in late autumn or early winter on heavy soil, leaving the ground rough for the snow and frost to break it down; light soils can be left until early spring. Every soil benefits from the addition of humus-forming material such as farmyard manure, peat, horse manure, leafmould, compost, straw, hop manure, seaweed, etc., dug into the top few inches. A month or so before planting, the soil should be broken down to a reasonable tilth and a top dressing of either bonemeal or a general fertilizer should be raked into the top couple of inches of soil.

Planting Out Dahlias can be grown either from tubers or green plants. Tubers are the roots which have formed

at the base of a plant grown the previous season. They can be planted from mid-April onwards. Space the tall types about 2½ ft. apart, the dwarf bedding types 1½ ft. apart, and the Lilliput types 1 ft. A stout 4 ft. stake or cane is needed for the taller types and these are put in position first. Plant the tubers 6 in. deep, just in front of the

'Twiggy', a good small decorative dahlia

cane. On poor soil put a couple of handfuls of a mixture of peat and a little general fertilizer into the hole and put the tuber on this, stem upwards, and fill in the hole with fine soil. Once the shoots appear above ground they are treated exactly as green plants.

Green plants are planted as soon as all danger of frost is over. Canes are put in position first and a hole slightly larger than the plant rootball is taken out just in front of the cane. A planting mixture of peat and fertilizer will help to get the plants away to a flying start on poor soil. Place the plant in the hole and fill it in with soil. Tie the plant loosely to the cane with soft twine then water the plants in well. Place a few slug pellets round each plant.

Summer Management For the first three or four weeks after planting, hoe the soil between the plants to keep down the weeds. When the plants have

developed five or six pairs of leaves, pinch out the growing tip to promote bushy growth. As the side shoots develop after this stopping they will need to be kept tied in to the cane.

The soil around the plants should never be allowed to dry out. Dahlias benefit greatly from the application of a mulch which will lessen the need for watering. Apply this in early July to a depth of about 4 in., completely covering the soil around the plants.

Flowering The first flowers should begin to appear about mid or late July. Better quality flowers can be obtained by disbudding, which means removing the two small side buds which appear either side of the main or terminal bud. Also remove the two side shoots which appear at the joint of the pair of leaves below the flowering bud. Left to themselves dahlias produce dozens of small poor quality flowers on short stems; a little light disbudding and de-shooting makes an amazing difference. Faded blooms should be removed to ensure continuation of flowering. This is particularly important with the single-flowering types which form seed heads very quickly. When cutting blooms for the house use a sharp knife, make a long slanting cut and plunge the stem immediately in deep water; cut in this way, dahlias should easily last a week. Cut as many blooms as you like, as often as you like.

Give the plants an occasional foliar feed. Make sure that all the plants to be saved for next year are clearly labelled with their name (if known), or type and colour.

Lifting and Storing
Lifting The tubers which have formed at the base of the plants will need to be lifted and stored for the winter. After the frost has killed the foliage cut through the main stem about 6 in. above soil level. With a fork loosen the soil round the tuber then push the fork underneath and lift the tuber.

Remove surplus soil from the roots and place them stem downwards in a greenhouse, shed, garage or spare room for about ten days to dry. While they are drying the tubers can be prepared for storage. Trim off the thin stringy roots from the ends of the tubers and cut the stem down to about 2 in. Any damaged ends of the roots should be trimmed away and the cut surface dusted with either green sulphur or a mixture of lime and flowers of sulphur in equal parts. Tie the label securely to the stem.

Storing If a frost-free garage, shed or spare room is available, place the tubers in shallow boxes of peat or dry soil. A cool cellar makes an ideal storage place. Where frost protection cannot be guaranteed, protect the tubers by placing them in stout wooden or cardboard boxes filled with an insulating material such as dry soil, sand, ashes, straw or sawdust.

Inspect the tubers once or twice while they are in store to make sure they are sound. Feel each tuber; if any parts are soft and brown this indicates rot which will have to be trimmed away, and the cut surface dusted with sulphur/lime powder. Any tubers with a white fluffy deposit (mildew) will need to be wiped clean with a dry cloth and dusted with sulphur/lime.

Propagation
Dahlias are very easy to propagate, whether from seed, division of tubers, or by cuttings.

Sowing Seed Plants will not reproduce true to type or colour from seed, except for the single Coltness type and the semi-double dwarf bedders. Sow the

seed in March in a heated greenhouse, thinly, in pans or boxes of John Innes seed compost or one of the soilless seed composts, covering the seed with $\frac{1}{4}$ in. of compost. Once they germinate they should be pricked out 24 to a box. Grow the plants on cool and in April move them to a cold frame to harden off before planting them out in late May or early June.

Dividing Tubers A dahlia tuber consists of a stem which is attached to the crown or collar where the eyes or buds are situated; swollen, potato-like tubers are attached to the crown. There are two types of tuber: the ground tuber is usually quite large and is formed at the base of a plant grown outdoors without restriction; the pot tuber is small and compact and is formed at the base of cuttings grown throughout the season in pots.

Before dividing the tuber the eyes must be visible and are coaxed into life by placing the tubers in moist peat or compost in late March or early April in shallow boxes which are placed either in a greenhouse or cold frame or on a sunny window-sill in the house. Once the eyes are visible, cut down the centre of the stem between the buds, right through the tuber. Further division may be possible, depending on the size of tuber and the position of the eyes, but each piece to be planted must contain a portion of stem attached to a piece of the crown bearing an eye, and at least one portion of swollen root or tuber. The divisions can either be planted out in mid-April or grown on in boxes in the greenhouse and planted out in late May.

Taking Cuttings Large numbers of cuttings can be taken from dahlia tubers; they root easily in a warm greenhouse in a minimum temperature

Left: A perfect pompon dahlia,

Right: Delphinium 'Mrs F. Bishop'

of 60°F (16°C). If any tubers show signs of rot or mildew, treat them as described earlier. The tubers are boxed up in moist peat or compost, or they can be bedded down on the open greenhouse bench, if possible, over some form of bottom heat. Keep the compost moist.

The cuttings are taken when the shoots are 3–4 in. long and are normally placed round the sides of a pot or pan or placed in a seed box in rows. With a clean sharp knife cut through the shoot just below the lowest leaf joint. Trim off the lower leaves, dip the end of the cutting in a hormone rooting powder then place the cutting 1 in. deep in the compost. Space the cuttings so that the leaves are just clear of each other and water lightly. Place the cuttings in a propagating frame, or bed the pots in moist peat on the open bench and provide shade.

Spray the cuttings with a fungicide to prevent damping off and after a day or so allow them a free flow of air. To lessen the risk of flagging, spray the cuttings with tepid water twice daily until rooting takes place in about 14 days.

Pot the rooted cuttings singly into $3\frac{1}{2}$-in. pots of J.I.P.1 or a peat-based compost. Keep the plants in a shady spot in the greenhouse for a day or so before placing them on a shelf near the glass, keeping the greenhouse well ventilated. In April remove the plants to a cold frame, keep the lights closed for a couple of days then progressively allow more ventilation until, towards planting out time in late May or, in the colder areas, in early June, the lights can be left off completely. At all times protect the plants from frost.

Delphiniums
July brings the delphinium flowers on towering spikes 5 to 7 ft. high, and the modern, shorter 4-ft. varieties which need little or no support. They also need rich soil for best results and in some gardens slugs can be a menace. From seed sown under glass in spring it is possible for some plants to flower in late summer, otherwise sow outdoors to obtain stock to flower freely the following year after transplanting.

A few strains come reasonably true such as the shorter-lived 'Pacific Hybrids'. Belladonna delphiniums, less tall with more open spikes, are in their way as attractive as the large-flowered varieties, though it is in the latter that double flowers occur. These hardy plants die to the ground in autumn and produce new shoots the following spring. They are used most frequently in herbaceous borders, mixed borders and in front of shrubs. Few flowers are so pure a blue; there are also many varieties with mauve, purple, violet, lilac or white flowers. Early in the 1960s the first hybrid reds, pinks and yellows were bred by Dr. R. A. H. Legro in Holland.

Generally described as hybrids of *D. elatum*, modern delphiniums are a mixture of more than half-a-dozen species. *D. belladonna* and its varieties are not so widely grown today. They produce several spikes on each main stem. *D. belladonna* tolerates light shade, but other delphiniums demand open, sunny positions, sheltered if possible from wind.

Soil Although a good garden loam is ideal, sandy or clay soils can be improved by digging in plenty of rotted manure, peat, leafmould, rotted compost or spent mushroom compost. Dig 18–20 in. deep, mix in 4 oz. per sq. yd. of a general fertilizer and let the ground settle for at least a month before planting.

Planting July to October, or March, are the best times to plant, except in heavy, wet ground or where slugs

Above left: 'Ann Miller'

Above: Summer delphiniums

abound, when spring is preferable. A space 2½ ft. across each way is sufficient in a border, but plants intended to produce spikes of exhibition quality deserve spaces 3–3½ ft. across. Young plants knocked from pots can be set with a trowel; those from open ground often arrive with their roots 'balled' in soil and then the roots must be spread out, keeping the crowns of the plants at surface level. Firm planting is essential.

Propagation Delphiniums are increased by seed, division and cuttings. Seed does not come true; that from a blue-flowered plant may produce seedlings with mauve, purple and white flowers. However, the best quality seed produces excellent plants cheaply. For preference sow freshly harvested seed in August or early September, in seed boxes filled with J.I. seed compost. Stand the boxes in a frame, greenhouse or sheltered spot outdoors. By late April or May seedlings are big enough to plant 1 ft. apart in a nursery bed outdoors and are moved later to their permanent positions.

Named varieties will come true only when propagated by dividing clumps in early spring, when the shoots are 3–4 in. high, or by cuttings. The roots are teased apart and the crown severed with a knife so each new portion has roots and one or two shoots. Cuttings generally produce sturdier plants. They

are made by choosing healthy shoots 3–4 in. high, scraping soil from around them before cutting them off close to the crown. Strip off their lower leaves, dip the lower ends of the stems in water, then in hormone rooting powder and set them with a dibber, about five in a 4½-in. pot of cutting compost. Bury one third of each stem, water the cuttings, and place them in a propagating case, or on a shaded greenhouse bench. They root in six to eight weeks and then are potted up singly in 3½-in. pots of J.I.P.1.

Cultivation In early spring crowns should be covered with ashes or coarse grit to keep slugs off the young shoots. Thin these out to leave the strongest four to six per plant, when 6 in. tall. Knock in a 6–8 ft. cane beside each shoot; tie the stems to the canes as they grow. Feed each plant with a heaped trowelful of dried blood in May, the same amount of general fertilizer in early June, and a tablespoon of sulphate of potash as the flower buds show colour, watering in these plant foods. Keep the soil damp. Dead flower spikes should be cut back; secondary spikes sometimes develop and bloom in early autumn.

Larkspur

(Hardy Annual Delphiniums) 1½–3 ft. Seed of annual delphiniums sown in March or April will produce flowering plants by about mid-July. Seedlings do not transplant well, therefore sow where the plants are to flower. For earlier flowering sow in the open in the autumn. The colour range includes shades of pink, lavender, mauve, rosy-scarlet and white and there are dwarf varieties (1½ ft.). The 3-ft. tall kinds with branching stock-flowered spikes are admirable for cutting.

Dianthus

Pinks (Half-hardy Annual) 9–18 in. Seed of the annual varieties of carnations and pinks, such as Chabaud carnations (*D. caryophyllus*) and the Japanese pink (*D. chinensis* 'Heddewigii') and others should be sown thinly in pots and lightly covered with sifted soil. Do this in February or March and place the pots in a warm greenhouse where germination should be evident in a week or ten days. Propagate by layering or cuttings.

Dianthus (*Caryophyllaceae*)

This rock plant is a large and valuable genus of easily grown, lime and sun-

Dianthus deltoides, the maiden pink, a fine rock garden plant

loving plants. Their colourful, often sweetly scented flowers are borne in summer. Propagate by division, cuttings, and seeds of those which are not hybrids. Many are fertile hybrids; seedlings of these will not come true but may produce some worth-while plants. *D. alpinus* makes low pads of dark green leaves and huge, almost stemless, rich pink flowers; *D. arvernensis* consists of ash-grey hummocks of leaves and 4-in. stems carrying rounded pink flowers. There is also a lovely white form. *D. caesius,* the Cheddar pink, has narrow grey leaves and large pink flowers on 6–9 in. stems; *D. deltoides,* the maiden pink, 9 in., makes sheets of flowers varying from light to dark pink; there is also a white form; D. 'Pike's Pink' is very dwarf with large pink flowers over flat cushions of grey-green leaves; *D. subacaulis* forms green mats and has slender 4-in. stems carrying neat rose-red flowers.

Diseases and Pests

Vegetables growing in fertile, well-drained and well-cultivated gardens seldom suffer greatly from pests and diseases. The modern gardener accepts that all wildlife has a right to live. It is only when things get out of hand that any living creature causing damage to garden plants can be rated as a pest. It is up to the gardener to use his superior intelligence to outwit possibly harmful small creatures instead of polluting the environment surrounding his home. The labels of packaged pesticides should be read carefully. If the contents are dangerous to you, your children and your family pets consider carefully before you buy such substances. Always lock dangerous pesticides quite safely away from children. Do *not* mix dangerous pesticides with water and store them in beer or lemonade bottles. Your child may drink the stuff and be poisoned. The commonly recommended insecticide nicotine, for example, is a poison. As for chemical weed killers the long term effect of some modern kinds is as yet unknown. The older weedkiller, sodium chlorate, is liable to explode; it also runs in the soil and may kill plants in your neighbours' gardens. Many sprays and powders contain derris or pyrethrum. These are natural insecticides prepared from plants. They are harmless to all warm-blooded creatures but derris can kill fish. If you use derris pesticides, keep sprays and dusts away from your garden pool. Encourage natural predators, e.g., the hedgehog, toad, frog, ladybird, wasps (in spring but not in summer) and lacewing flies. Learn to distinguish between the helpful centipede, the less helpful millepede and the unpleasant wireworm. Most moths, butterflies and their caterpillars are on your side. The caterpillars of cabbage white butterflies and of the cabbage moth are not! The following list gives some of the most common pests and diseases, the chief vegetables affected, the damage done, and lastly the control measures available.

Aphids (greenfly, mealy aphis, blackfly)
Vegetable: all. *Damage:* they are sap suckers. Plants are weakened, leaves die and flower buds may be ruined. *Control:* allow plants sufficient space and do not grow vegetables in shade. Water well and often in dry, summer weather. Keep down weeds, Encourage ladybirds. Spray with derris or pyrethrum.

Birds
Vegetable: seed beds and the seedlings of several vegetables. *Damage:* seeds are sought for and devoured; seedlings are pecked. *Control:* net or protect with black cotton. A scarecrow or strips of tinfoil may be tried.

Cabbage Root Fly
Vegetable: the cabbage tribe. *Damage:* grubs burrow into the roots; plants wilt and die. *Control:* set out transplants in firm soil and mulch with garden compost.

Carrot Root Fly
Vegetable: carrot. *Damage:* grubs eat roots; plants yellow and die. *Control:* thin seedlings only when soil is moist. Bury unwanted thinnings and broken foliage.

Caterpillars
Vegetable: the cabbage tribe. *Damage:* leaves are eaten. *Control:* pick off caterpillars. Spray with derris or with salt solution (2 oz. of table salt to one gallon of cold water).

Celery Fly
Vegetable: celery. *Damage:* maggots burrow into the leaves which appear blistered. A bad attack can lead to dead leaves and a poor crop. *Control:* hand pick and burn 'blistered' leaves. Dig deeply in winter to expose pupae to birds. Spray seedlings with derris in May and June.

Club Root
Vegetable: the cabbage tribe. *Damage:* the fungus causes swellings on the roots which decay. Plants are stunted and may die. *Control:* do not raise plants in soil known to be infected with the fungus. Rotate crops. Feed the soil with plenty of compost. Lime where necessary. Burn roots of affected plants.

Club root of brassicas
Left: a clean root. Right: an affected root

Common Scab
Vegetable: potato. *Damage:* scabby marks on the skin. *Control:* seldom serious. Do not lime ground in which potatoes are to be planted. Rotate crops. Surround seed tubers with peat, leaf-mould or lawn mowings at planting time.

Cutworms

Vegetable: many. *Damage*: these soil caterpillars eat stems, leaves and roots. They often cut stems of seedlings at soil level. *Control*: destroy any found when digging. Hoe frequently and destroy any seen. Keep down weeds. Encourage blackbirds and thrushes.

Cutworm

Damping Off

Vegetable: many at seedling stage in greenhouse and in frames. *Damage*: a fungus which causes stems to shrivel. Seedlings topple over and die. *Control*: use sterile composts when sowing seeds. Sow thinly. Do not over-water, prick out early, ventilate freely. Cheshunt Compound is a chemical control.

Grey Mould

Vegetable: lettuce, marrow, melon, cucumber, tomato. *Damage*: a fungal disease. Softening of plant tissue is followed by decay. Outgrowths of grey mould appear. *Control*: ventilate well. Clear away any debris. Remove side shoots when quite small. Prune cleanly so that no jagged stems are left. Allow plants sufficient room. Do not splash plants when watering. Dust with flowers of sulphur or spray with colloidal sulphur.

Leaf Mould

Vegetable: tomato (in greenhouse). *Damage*: this fungus shows as yellow spots on upper surfaces of leaves with pale greyish mould on undersides. *Control*: ventilate well. Give plants adequate space. Do not over-water. Remove and burn infected foliage. Spray with zineb or a copper-based fungicide.

Leather Jackets

Vegetable: many. *Damage*: grubs feed on plant roots just below ground level. *Control*: as for cutworms.

Mildew

Vegetable: many. *Damage*: the fungus shows as a grey/white powder on foliage. *Control*: ensure that plants have sufficient moisture and ventilate frames and greenhouses well. Dust with flowers of sulphur. Spray with zineb.

Millepedes

Vegetable: all. *Damage*: roots are eaten. *Control*: destroy any found when digging and cultivating. Remove all rubbish to the compost heap. Trap by burying pieces of sliced potato or carrot on skewers in the soil. This pest prefers roots already decaying. Do not confuse with beneficial centipedes.

Millepede (left) and centipede

Mosaic Virus

Vegetable: vegetable marrow. *Damage*: leaves show mottling and distortion. Plants are dwarfed. Crop is poor. Plants die. *Control*: prevent by spraying plants with derris or pyrethrum to deter aphids which spread the disease. Destroy plants of white bryony. Pull up and burn affected plants.

Onion Fly

Vegetable: onion, sometimes leek and shallots. *Damage*: grubs eat roots and below ground portion of plants. *Control*: avoid breaking or bruising onion foliage. Thin onion seedlings only when soil is damp. Bury broken onion foliage and unwanted thinnings.

Parsnip Canker

Vegetable: parsnip. *Damage*: brown patches occur on the parsnips. Rot may also occur. *Control*: seldom serious. Grow resistant parsnips, e.g. 'Avonresister'.

Pea and Bean Weevils

Vegetable: peas, beans. *Damage*: Leaves of seedlings are eaten. The bites show as 'U'-shaped notches. *Control*: hoe regularly around seedlings to disturb the pests. Break down clods under which they hide. Remove all rubbish to the compost heap. Dust or spray with derris.

Pea Moth

Vegetable: peas. *Damage*: grubs eat peas in the pods. *Control*: rotate crops. Hoe frequently around plants to expose pupae in the ground to birds. Keep well watered in dry spells and spray with water when pods are forming. Early sowings often escape this pest.

Potato Blight

Vegetable: potatoes, tomatoes. *Damage*: the fungus shows as brown/black markings on foliage. Potatoes and tomatoes decay. Plants rot and smell. *Control*: where this disease makes potato growing hazardous grow only first early varieties. Some newer varieties appear to resist blight. 'Pentland Crown' is an example. 'Maris Peer' foliage can suffer from the disease but the tubers may not be harmed. It seldom occurs on tomato plants in the greenhouse. Spray or dust with Bordeaux mixture or a fungicide from early July onwards.

Saddleback

Vegetable: onion. *Damage*: underside of bulb splits. *Control*: never permit plants to become dry at the roots when bulbs are swelling.

Slugs and Snails

Vegetable: all. *Damage*: these pests eat foliage, roots, tubers and fruits. *Control*: remove all rubbish. Search for possible hiding places and destroy the pests. Bait slugs by leaving cabbage and lettuce leaves on the soil at night. Encourage hedgehogs, toads, frogs, slow worms and song birds.

Turnip Flea Beetles

Vegetable: the cabbage tribe, radish, swede, turnip. *Damage*: holes show in younger leaves. *Control*: use proprietary slug killers with care. Some are harmful to pets and wild life. Prepare seed beds properly. Remove all rubbish. Keep seedlings well-watered in dry spring and summer weather. Dust seedlings with derris. The damage usually looks nastier than it is.

Turnip Gall Weevil

Vegetable: the cabbage tribe, swede, turnip. *Damage*: grubs occur in galls on roots and stems just below soil surface. *Control*: very common but causes little if any damage. Unsightly. Burn badly infested roots. Do not confuse with club root.

Wireworm

Vegetable: all. *Damage*: grubs eat roots. *Control*: when starting a new garden do not dig in turves or couch grass. Trap by burying cut pieces of potato or carrot on skewers. Search when digging and hoeing and kill any found. Grow less vulnerable vegetables such as broad beans and members of the cabbage family if this pest is present in quantity in a new garden.

Wireworm

Fruit Pests

Birds Pests are, alas, always with us but thanks to modern specifics there is generally no reason why they should cause serious damage to our trees and crops. There is, however, one exception against which no easy defence has yet been discovered – the birds which, it must be admitted, often add much to the enjoyment of our gardens but can rob us of our reward for a year's care in a few hours.

As they begin to ripen, nearly all fruits are subject to bird attack but, worse than that, our chances of any crop at all can be destroyed the previous winter when birds turn to the dormant buds on gooseberries, currants, plums and other tree fruits as a source of food in hard weather. Which fruits are most liable to be attacked probably depends on the balance between the trees available and the local bird population.

To protect the buds one can apply a proprietary bird repellent spray. This can work well, for a time, but frequent renewal can be expensive and is a task easily forgotten. More lasting protection is provided by rayon web, the fine gossamer strands of which are teased out over the tree or bush. The birds hate this material but the individual threads are so fine and fragile they cause no injuries as cotton and, particularly, nylon thread can.

The only absolute protection against birds is provided by small mesh netting carefully draped over permanent or temporary supports. Plastic netting is available in many sizes and is rot-proof and very light in weight.

Both rayon web and netting will, of course, protect the ripening crops as well as the buds in winter.

Aphids   Like birds, aphids (the greenfly tribe) always make an appearance sooner or later. If unchecked they can do serious damage to the tree fruits. Although they do little apparent harm to strawberries and raspberries, their sap sucking introduces virus disease which can be fatal. Aphids tend to attack growing points first and their activities frequently cause leaves to curl. Aphids over-winter in the egg stage on the trees.

Woolly aphid

Caterpillars   A number, notably the leaf and fruit-eating tortrix caterpillars

and those of the winter moths (known as 'loopers') feed on fruit trees, particularly apples, pears, plums and gooseberries. The parent moths lay their eggs in bark crevices between October and March.

Capsids   These bugs hatch in spring from eggs over-wintered on the tree. They first eat the leaves and then start on the fruitlets. Apples are the most common sufferers but currants and gooseberries are attacked by related species.

Sawflies   These creatures lay their eggs in the flower of the apple or, less frequently, pear. The larva bores into the fruitlet. It will pass from one to another, spoiling each, and then fall to the ground. A mass of sticky frass (excreta) exudes from the hole where the pest enters the fruit.

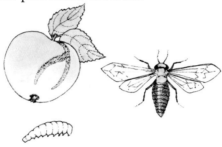

Apple sawfly (left) and Plum sawfly

Codling Moths   This moth lays its eggs in early summer on leaves or fruit, and the grubs bore into the fruit to feed. These are the creatures you may find near the core when you come to eat the apple. Pears are less commonly attacked.

Codling moth

Spraying Programme   There are many other pests to spoil our fruit but the above-mentioned are those which do most damage. A drenching of the dormant trees and bushes in winter with tar-oil will do much to kill over-wintering eggs but should only be resorted to about one winter in three because it also kills friendly insects which prey on red spider mites which may then become a menace.

A minimum spray programme starts at the green cluster stage of apples and pears to kill caterpillars and greenfly. Give a second spraying at the pink bud

stage (apples) or white bud stage (pears), to deal with capsids, and a third spraying as soon as 90% of the blossom petals have fallen, to kill sawfly and tortrix caterpillars. In mid-June spray to deal with codling moth and tortrix caterpillars, repeating this a fortnight later. Two sprayings are essential for plums – between bud burst and the white bud stage, to control aphids and caterpillars, when the petals have fallen and the fruitlets set, against sawfly.

Further sprayings, of course, must be given if pests are seen. Aphids may appear at any time and if the fruit is shortly to be eaten it is essential to spray with something which is non-toxic to humans – derris, for example.

There are dozens of pesticides on offer in the garden shops. The labels on the bottles or packets will tell you what pests they are intended for and when and how to apply them. The important thing is to follow those directions exactly.

Fruit Diseases

Careful attention at all times to garden hygiene will do much to keep disease to a minimum. Indeed, one cannot 'cure' plant diseases and prevention must always be the policy. Always cut out any dead branches or shoots as soon as you notice them and burn them. Also burn any rotting fruits.

Scab   This fungoid disease disfigures the skin of many apples and pears, especially in wetter and more humid districts. It is not likely to cause much harm if you spray regularly with captan at the green cluster, pink (or white) bud and petal fall stages.

Brown Rot   Concentric rings of small pustules on ripe or ripening fruit are the outward signs of this fungus. It is very contagious. Burn all infected fruit and wash your hands immediately after touching them.

Brown rot

Silver Leaf   This may attack all stone fruits (and sometimes apples) but is particularly virulent on plums. The leaves assume a silvery tinge and the diagnosis is confirmed by a brown stain inside the wood of infected branches or shoots. The disease is spread by spores entering wounds or cuts in the bark, usually between September and May. Do not, therefore, prune in winter and cut out any dead or infected wood in midsummer. Pare all wounds smooth and cover with a protective tree-pruning paint.

Leaf Curl A very common trouble with apricots, peaches and nectarines, causing the young leaves to become puckered and curled. Such leaves become yellow, then reddish and develop 'blisters'. New growth is distorted.

The most likely means of control is to spray with lime-sulphur in late February or early March while growth is still dormant and just before the buds swell. Repeat in autumn just before the leaves fall. Once growth has begun in spring lime-sulphur must not be used; instead spray with captan.

Virus Diseases Of recent years a number of fruit troubles have been found to be of virus origin. Those most likely to come to the amateur grower's notice are those which attack strawberries and raspberries, drastically reducing crop yields. To avoid virus troubles only buy new stock from a nurseryman who takes part in the Government Certification Scheme, and spray against aphids.

Early symptoms include various leaf markings but these can easily be mistaken for those caused by mineral deficiency. If you see abnormal markings on the leaves of strawberries or raspberries, give first-aid in the shape of foliar watering with a foliar feed containing chelated trace minerals just in case the trouble is due only to a lack of iron or magnesium or other trace element. Never use suspected plants for propagation. If cropping fails, dig up and burn the offenders.

Erica
Heath

There are many species and almost countless garden forms of heath. All like open situations and do best in lighter soils. They may be lightly clipped over after flowering. Kinds can be had to flower in almost every month of the year. Some will grow on light, acid soil only, while a few others will grow where lime is present.

The principal species, of which well-known variants are cultivated, are: *E. carnea* (evergreen, low growing shrub, lime tolerant), flowering from early winter to early spring, the colours range from white through pink to purple; *E. cinerea* (evergreen, low growing shrub, will not grow on chalk), the native purple bell heather with flowers mostly ranging from white through pink to purple, from June to September.

The numerous forms of these will be more than adequate for most gardens and will provide colour throughout the year. Those who wish to make a heath garden will find that many other kinds are available.

Euphorbia
Spurge

This vast genus includes a few good garden plants. All have bracts sur-rounding clustered flower heads. *E. charassias* and *E. veneta* (syn. *E. wulfenii*), are sub-shrubs, with year round blue-grey, somewhat succulent foliage, and build up into imposing plants 3 ft. high or more till they burst into almost a fountain of sulphur-yellow heads of flower in spring. They look well with shrubs or on a wall. One of the best of all spring-flowering herbaceous plants is *E. polychroma* (syn. *E. epithymoides*), 20 in., a sturdy, compact plant which produces heads of bright sulphur-yellow bracts in April and early May. *E. griffithii* 'Fireflow', 2½ ft., produces deep fiery heads in May and June. Of the more vigorous species, which have their uses as ground coverers, *E. cyparissias*, 10 in., spreads rapidly and has bluish-grey foliage and heads of sulphur-yellow. *E. amygdaloides* and *E. robbiae* are similar, with deep green foliage and a reasonable spread, but are more suitable among shrubs than in a perennial border. The most popular and widely grown greenhouse species is *E. pulcherrima*, the poinsettia, which is so showy in autumn and winter.

Keep plants in full light and moderately watered. A temperature of 60–65°F (16–18°C) is ideal. Once the bracts expand less moisture is needed. At the end of April, soak the roots and cut back stems to 4 in. From these will develop three or four shoots, which can be used as cuttings. Dip the cut ends in powdered charcoal before inserting in a mixture of loam, peat and sand. Provide a temperature of about 60°F (16°C) and when plenty of roots have formed, feed with liquid manure.

Below and right: Poinsettia (Euphorbia pulcherrima) does well in a living room and is at its best in winter

Below: Erica carnea thrive on soils containing chalk or lime

F₁ Hybrids

This term frequently appears on seed packets and in seed catalogues. It signifies that the variety is produced by crossing two selected parents. Plants of the two selected parents are grown in separate blocks. Pollen from the male flowers of one parent is transferred to flowers of the second parent. Self-fertilization of the flowers of the second (female) parent is prevented. Seed has to be produced afresh each year and the cross pollination is effected by hand. F₁ hybrid seeds are, therefore, usually dearer. In favour of F₁ hybrids is their outstanding vigour. The plants also have striking uniformity. This fact is worth noting if you exhibit at local or national shows. It is not easy to find several vegetables which are almost identical and just what is wanted for the show bench. Flowers are of more intense colour and larger than ordinary hybrid seedlings. It is, however, a long and expensive process to obtain such seed, therefore it costs more per packet. Also the complicated breeding programme has to be repeated, as seed saved from F₁ hybrids grown in the garden, would prove far from reliable.

Fences

Fencing has an important role to play in the garden where it can be used to provide shelter from strong winds, privacy from neighbours and a means of dividing off or partitioning parts of the garden. Quite often, a suitably selected fence can add considerable character and interest in a garden and it is one possible solution to the problem of concealing an ugly view.

There are several different designs or patterns available and the choice of timber usually lies between cedar, pine or larch, and other materials are concrete and plastic. The type of pattern will have a bearing on the amount of protection or privacy afforded. For example, a solid or close-boarded fence with adequate overlaps will provide much more privacy than a more open interwoven design. Some such fences have a special 'peep-proof' finish where extra intermediate battens are supplied which, when nailed to the overlap timber, prevents them opening up eventually. Adequate overlap of the timber used in the fill-in part of the fence also ensures privacy and very good protection from winds.

Fence height is a matter for personal decision. For complete privacy and shelter, the highest fence should be selected and this will usually be about 6 ft. The general range of heights is 6 ft., 5½ ft., 5 ft., 4½ ft., 4 ft., 3½ ft. Sections are usually 6 ft. wide.

A fence is only as strong as its supports and the way in which they are inserted in the ground. They should, in most cases, be about 3 ft. taller than the fence if the fence is 6 ft. high. For lower fences the posts can be about 2 ft. taller. The posts must be buried from about 2 to 3 ft. in the ground, allowing for the posts to extend about 3–4 in. above the top rail of the fence panel to accommodate the post cap.

The erection of a fence should start by placing a garden line along the site. Several posts should be laid down on the ground, close to this line, spacing them apart according to the width of the fence panels (1). The holes can then be excavated for the posts. Treat the bottom of each post with preservative to a point above soil level (2).

Place the first post in position and retain it in place with a few bricks, etc. The exact position for the next post is now determined by fastening a fence panel to this first post (3). The next post can be placed in the hole and the panel fixed to this (4). Work proceeds in this way until the fence has been erected. When several posts are in place, they can be cemented in (5). Take the precaution of fixing a temporary stay or support to each post to prevent movement while the cement is setting.

Concrete posts will ensure a rot-proof fence erection and, in many cases, these can be ordered specially. Some firms can supply concrete spurs or stub-posts which are cemented in the hole first and then a length of wooden fence post is bolted onto this. The stub-posts stand above ground level and the base of the wooden post which is attached to it is kept off the soil.

Ferns

Ferns like occasional overhead sprayings of tepid rain water, but do not spray those species with hairy foliage. Moist, well-drained compost containing plenty of leafmould plus some bonemeal is suitable.

Dust-like spores form on the undersides of the fronds; when sown these form a prothallus, which contains male and female organs, which, in a temperature of 50–55°F (10–13°C), fertilize to produce the first frond.

Specimens for the cool greenhouse include: *Adiantum cuneatum*, the maidenhair fern; *Nephrolepis exaltata* – for hanging baskets; *Pteris cristata* and *Davallia dissecta*.

The Garden Frame

Types There are three standard patterns of frames, determined by the size of the glass or light. The English frame is 6 ft. long × 4 ft. wide, usually glazed with four sheets of glass each measuring 18 in. × 12 in. A smaller form measures 4 ft. × 3 ft. and is easy to handle. The Dutch frame measures 59 in. × 31¾ in. and is glazed with a single pane of glass. The French frame measures 4 ft. 4 in. × 4 ft. 5 in.

Sectional frames of cast aluminium or steel are on the market, and there are many satisfactory portable frames with single or span roofs, with sliding tops easily removed for ready access.

The size of frame you buy or make will depend on the purpose for which it is to be used, although the aim should be to have one as large as space and pocket allow. Many frames are made with 4 ft. extensions, so that as with cloches, any length of run can be achieved.

Position Where possible place the frame due south and not under or too near trees. If it can be backed on to the greenhouse or other building to give protection from north winds, so much the better.

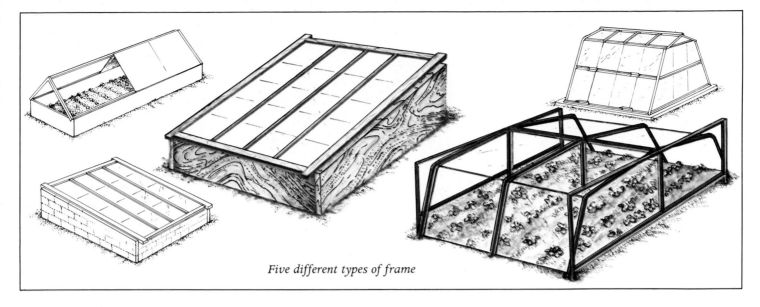

Five different types of frame

The body of the frame can be of tongued and grooved timber, brick, breeze blocks or metal. Where frames are not permanent constructions make sure they are on a proper draught and damp-proof base. Provide a firm path round the structure, otherwise it will be difficult to attend to plants in winter or wet weather.

Keep the glass clean and free from cracks with puttying so efficient that rain drips cannot penetrate. Make sure the frame will open and shut properly without water getting between the panes or hinge joints.

Water with care to avoid excess moisture in the frame. An old-fashioned remedy for keeping out dampness is to place a lump of quicklime under each light. This takes up air moisture in winter and lasts for several weeks.

Heat escapes through the bottom of the frame into the surrounding soil. A 2–3-in. deep bed of cinders placed under the frame area before soil is added, greatly reduces the loss.

Propagating frames are used exclusively for raising plants from seed or cuttings. They can be a simple arrangement, such as a box on which a sheet of glass is placed, or a more elaborate structure with a wooden or metal base.

Hardening Off Frames are invaluable for hardening off greenhouse-raised plants such as summer bedding plants, which must be gradually acclimatized to outdoor conditions. At times greenhouses become overcrowded and the frame can be used to accommodate plants in different stages of development – an important matter when they are being grown for living room or other domestic decoration.

Heating Frames can be electrically heated by soil cables which should be laid on 2 in. of sand and covered with another 2 in. before loamy soil is put on. Make sure there is no crossing or touching by different sections of the same heating element.

Ventilation Damp and draughts cannot be kept out simply by keeping the top closed. Without air, mildew and rotting will occur. Ventilation is needed daily except in very cold or frosty weather. Never let cold winds blow into a frame; sliding lights are better than the hinged type since they can always be kept open away from the wind by using little blocks. Protective mats are valuable during frosty periods but should not be used when they are wet. It is an advantage to have duplicate mats so that the wet ones can be dried.

Forcing With heat you can force chicory, rhubarb and seakale, and in January, early potatoes 'Home Guard' and 'Arran Pilot' can be planted. Lettuce sown in September will heart by Christmas, while partially grown lettuce, cauliflower and endive plants can be placed in frames to mature. Parsley transferred to frames in October will give winter pickings. Continuous supplies of mustard and cress may be had by successional sowings.

Drying Frames can be used for drying onions, potatoes and haricot beans, while they keep dry the ripening seed heads of onions and leeks.

Catch Cropping You can use the frame for catch cropping; for instance early tulips planted 4 in. deep in early November overplanted with October-sown lettuce 'Trocadero'; 'Early French Breakfast' radish sown between the plants in January, will mature before the lettuce or tulips are very large.

A Greenhouse Annexe Frames can serve as an annexe to a greenhouse to accommodate flowering plants out of bloom and those for which the greenhouse would be too warm in summer.

Fruit Trees

The nutritional value of a plentiful supply of fresh fruit cannot be overestimated and in these inflationary days an investment in fruit trees and bushes will save you money year after year.

For many gardeners, however, the greatest joy of home fruit-growing lies not so much in cash-saving, horticultural interest or visual effect, as in the enhanced flavour of fresh fruit eaten direct from the plant.

The provision of a special plot reserved entirely for fruit is the ideal. This enables you to group together fruits having similar manurial needs – gooseberries and red currants close to the apples, for instance, as these all call for much potash, and blackcurrants next to plums and pears, these three requiring more nitrogen than the first trio.

Having all your fruit in one place also simplifies spraying and makes it easier to provide protection from birds. However, this is not always possible and growing fruit in amongst the flower beds is a satisfactory alternative.

A wall provides shelter and warmth and, therefore, sometimes enables less hardy fruits to be grown successfully. A tree trained against a wall can be more easily given temporary covering in the event of spring frost and can very

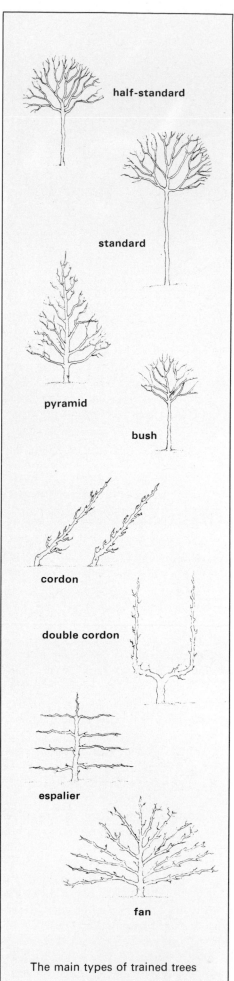

half-standard

standard

pyramid

bush

cordon

double cordon

espalier

fan

The main types of trained trees

easily be netted over to keep off birds. A tree growing against a house wall, being so close at hand, often receives better attention than those at the other end of the garden.

What to Grow Fruits are normally divided into two main classes: (1) The soft fruits which include herbaceous plants such as strawberries, the shrubby ones, such as blackcurrants and gooseberries, and the cane fruits, such as raspberries and blackberries. All these are grown on their own roots. (2) The top or tree fruits. Apples, pears and plums are common examples. The named varieties you buy at a nursery have all been budded or grafted (mostly the former) on to roots (known as the rootstock) raised separately and designed to impart certain desired characteristics to the behaviour of the tree. Thus for garden planting apples are frequently budded on a weak-growing rootstock which will result in the tree starting to fruit early in life and never growing too big.

Tree fruits may be pruned or trained to various different shapes or forms, e.g.:

Standard

This is the old-fashioned bushy-topped tree with a vertical stem of 6 ft. before the lowest branches arise.

Half-standard

As above, but with a stem of only 4 ft.

A half-standard, therefore, is only 2 ft. shorter than a full standard and both types are too large for most gardens. Not only do such trees eventually take up much space (30–40 ft. each way) but a ladder is essential for spraying, pruning and picking, and a good crop (possibly over 200 lb. of apples) is probably greater than any one family wants of one variety. Half-standard plums of the varieties whose branches tend to 'weep' downwards (such as 'Warwickshire Drooper') are sometimes planted in gardens but such a tree still requires from 15–20 ft. each way.

Bush

This is the most common form of tree, with a clear stem of from 1½ to 3 ft. below the branches. Soft fruits are also grown as bushes, the clear stem of red and white currants and gooseberries being about 6 in. Blackcurrants are grown as bushes but with no leg, the branches being encouraged to grow from as low down as possible. Apples are sometimes grafted or budded on weak-growing rootstocks which result in quite a small tree. Dwarf bushes are very suitable for garden planting.

Cordon

A single-stemmed tree without branches, fruiting spurs arising directly

Harvest from the fruit garden

from the main stem. To induce early fruiting, cordons are frequently planted at an angle of 45° and are then referred to as oblique cordons. This is a useful type for the small garden and enables a range of different varieties to be planted in a small space, thus spreading the season of use and reducing the risk of poor cropping because of inadequate cross-pollination. Single vertical cordons are useful for growing against house walls, filling in comparatively narrow spaces between windows, etc. Pears especially do very well in such places.

Double Cordon

This is formed by training the stem horizontally on both sides of the short vertical stem or cordon from the extremity of each 'arm' so that the tree is U-shaped. In a similar way a triple cordon can be trained with three main vertical stems. The double or triple cordon shape is most often used with gooseberries and redcurrants.

Espalier

A tree with a central vertical stem from which horizontal branches spring in pairs, one on each side. Apples and pears are often grown in this form alongside paths but espaliers are also useful for training against walls particularly where space for upward extension is limited.

Fan

From a short vertical leg the branches are trained like the ribs of a fan, all in one plane. Fans are often trained against walls but they can equally well be freestanding but fastened to horizontal wires. Fans are most usually formed from peaches, nectarines, apricots, pears and plums, but apples can be trained in this form, against horizontal wires.

Pyramid

A Christmas-tree shaped tree, with a central vertical stem from which the branches radiate. Apple and pear pyramids on dwarfing rootstocks are excellent for the small garden. Although there are no dwarfing rootstocks for plums, pyramid-training is gaining in popularity for keeping garden plum trees within bounds.

Family Tree

This term does not indicate a shape but means that several varieties have been grafted together to form one tree. The 'family trees' sold commercially are usually in the form of bushes, but this is not absolutely essential.

Fuchsias

Fuchsias are shrubs and in mild districts the hardiest kinds, such as *F. magellanica* and its variety *riccartonii*, are used for hedges. But most of the hybrid forms grown are not so hardy and are treated as disposable bedding plants or plants for a cool greenhouse. They are readily trained as bushes, cascades, standards and other more elaborate shapes. Their interesting hanging flowers are varied in size, form and colour and there is a multitude of varieties, of differing habit.

Propagation Soft wood cuttings root readily. Those of hardy kinds are taken in spring, as are also those of greenhouse ones needed for making standards or pyramids or small plants to flower later the same year, but the bulk of greenhouse ones are made in midsummer for growing through the winter in a minimum temperature of 55°F (13°C) to flower from May onwards. Soft wood cuttings are made by removing the top few inches of a soft grow-

Above right: Fuchsia 'Display', a single-flowered kind suitable for bedding out and (below) 'Golden Marinka'

ing shoot. Ideally such a shoot should not have flower buds, but as the tip will be pinched out (stopped) soon after rooting this is not essential. The stem is cut with a razor blade straight across just below a node (leaf joint) and the bottom two pairs of leaves are carefully removed. The base is dipped in a hormone rooting powder and pushed into the cutting bed or pot, containing pure sand or a mixture of two parts of sand and one of peat, which gives better results as the brittle roots are less liable to be broken when removed for potting. Cuttings will normally root in 3–4 weeks and should be potted singly into 3-in. pots of J.I.P.1 or a soilless compost. As soon as they are growing again freely the top of each plant is removed, leaving only the two bottom pairs of leaves.

After-care When the pots are full of roots the plants are moved into a larger size with a richer mixture, until by the end of the winter the summer-rooted plants will have reached their flowering size pots and be in J.I.P.3. Standards and other top-heavy plants must be in a loam-based compost to help keep them stable.

Stopping During the summer shoots may be shortened to two nodes again and again to make a bushy plant. However, as it takes six weeks from stopping to flowering on a side shoot, do not go on stopping too long. Cuttings destined to be trained as standards should be stopped once. The best side shoots are then tied to a cane, the others removed.

Standards The best standards are not made from the stiff upright types but from the vigorous growing pendulous ones, therefore the trunk of the standard needs to be tied in straight at all stages. To make a head on top of a given length of trunk grow the stem at least two or three further nodes and then rub out the top. The growth from the nodes make branches from which the head is formed as if it were a bush. Side shoots which appear lower down should be rubbed out at once, but the leaves growing from the trunk should be left to make food for growth.

Half standards make good table decorations in a sun parlour, but fuchsias do not like being moved into overheated, draughty or poorly lit places and usually drop their flower buds. They are fine in window boxes and on terraces and patios, as well as bedded out, preferably in beds by themselves.

Hanging Baskets The pendulous varieties, known as basket or cascade forms, are stopped as for bushes, but put the pots on other inverted pots to keep the growth above the bench. Or the plants can be grown in hanging baskets suspended from greenhouse rafters, or from the rafters of patio, porch or pergola or a bracket from a wall.

Planting The soft growth of even the hardy fuchsias will be killed by frost but new shoots will usually shoot up from below the ground the following year. When planting scoop out a shallow depression in which to put the plant and after it is growing well gradually return the earth so that the base of the stem becomes covered then in autumn put on a good top dressing. The small mound will help to protect the basal buds.

Housing Plants to be housed during the winter in a frost-proof place should be lifted immediately frost has cut the leaves, and stored almost dry until March when they will start into growth if moved into warmth and watered.

Gladioli

The gladiolus (correct plural gladioli in Britain, gladiolus in North America and elsewhere), is named from the bud-tip that breaks through the foliage and resembles the short broad blade of the Roman soldier's and gladiator's sword.

What is planted is not a bulb, but a corm, in which all parts of the eventual plant are present in embryo. Choose, therefore, large high-crowned corms feeling heavy for their width and with a small basal plate (root scar) underneath, indicating that they are young and vigorous. Ensure that these get a good start and are well fed from the beginning, since the number of buds to a spike is determined quite early. Grown mainly as cut flowers and for garden decoration, they vary from little over 1 in. to about 7 in. across the bloom.

Soils and Situations Gladioli will grow on most soils, but prefer a medium to light well-drained loam with plenty of humus and some rich, moisture-retaining material from 1½–2 ft. beneath.

Preferably, they should be sited where there will be full sun for most of the day and not close to trees or hedges.

Where to Grow In the herbaceous border they make good tall plants, not merely for the back, but to vary the centre. Here the foliage-fans create useful green verticals, even when the plant is not in flower.

Tubs or small beds may be planted, but tubs should be at least 15 in. deep. Underplanting with the usual range of low summer-flowering bedding-plants works well, as they feed at a different level. Never let the tubs dry out, but ensure there is ample drainage.

Preparing the Site Dig in the autumn, working plenty of water-holding material into the second spit or immediately below it. Rotted farmyard manure is best; but mature compost, leafmould, sedge-peat, or anything organic and

moisture-retentive will do. Gladioli like good drainage about the corms, but plenty of moisture at the roots. For the smaller types, heavy feeding is not required.

Gladioli grow best in neutral or slightly acid soil, so do not over-lime. In March make holes about 3 ft. apart throughout the patch, sprinkle a little naphthalene in, and cover immediately. The fumes will drive out wireworms. Avoid planting where potato ellworm is known to be present, as this attacks the corms and their roots. Douse the whole area with a weak solution of disinfectant, to which a liquid slug-killer may be added. Then sprinkle dry slug-bait around the plot.

Planting The spacing between corms should be sufficient for easy hoeing, not less than 7 in. Larger-flowered kinds should be set about 9 in. apart, medium-flowered 6 in., small-flowered, primulinus, and nanus hybrids, 4 in. Plant throughout April and May. For the closely placed ones, dig a narrow trench about 6 in. deep. For the widely spaced ones it is quicker to trowel out holes; never use a pointed

Gladioli: above: 'Green Woodpecker', right, the medium-flowered 'Daily Sketch'

Left: Fuchsia 'Mrs Popple'

Above right: a typical gladiolus corm, showing the base plate, the new corm and the cormlets

dibber that will create an air-pocket beneath the corm, as well as compacting the soil. On medium soils there should be 4½–5 in. of soil above each full-sized corm, on light soils 5–5½ in., on heavy soils 4 in.

Have a bucket of sharp fine sand to hand, into which has been thoroughly mixed a fungicide and an insecticidal dust. Dust trenches or holes with bonemeal or steamed boneflour to promote root development. Then place a handful of the sand mixture where each

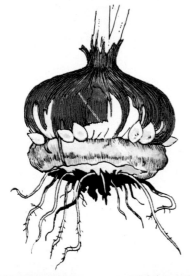

corm is to sit, press the corm firmly into this, and pour a second handful over it. This ensures good drainage around the corm, easy, dry lifting, and a protective barrier against below-soil pests and fungus growths. Fill the hole with crumbled, stone-free soil.

Before planting each corm, strip any remaining leaf-husks and examine the top. If you want the maximum number of spikes with a multiplication of corms harvested, leave all the little growing 'eyes' intact and be careful not to damage them when pressing the corm into the sand. If you want one straight spike, especially for exhibition purposes, rub out all but the most central 'eye'. *Never* plant corms that are stonehard, or squashy, or with large patches of brown, or with concentric circles of black where the old leaves joined. These will infect other stock with disease.

After-care Hand weed close to the plants in moist conditions; hoe between the rows in dry weather. Mulching will reduce this labour, help the soil to retain heat and moisture, and suppress weeds. Mulch after the plants are showing and the larger-flowered kinds have

been given a side-dressing of an organically-based fertilizer. Uproot entirely and destroy any gladioli showing yellow leaves with still-green veins. These are harbouring *Fusarium oxysporum*, which is incurable.

Watch for bud tips to appear and see that these grow clear of the foliage without getting crooked. Stake with bamboo canes in wind-swept areas and always for the larger-flowered varieties, as soon as the direction of facing can be determined by the forward bend of the flower head. Tie in with *soft* material.

Cutting Cut in the early morning when the first bloom is partly or fully open, using a sharp knife down inside the foliage and then slanting it through the stem, to leave at least four leaves intact. Treat the plant as a growing entity, so that about six weeks later you may lift the healthy new corm.

Lifting Trim off all roots and foliage immediately and dry the corms thoroughly and quickly. A fortnight later the old corms will pull cleanly away from the new ones, which should be cleaned, further dried, dusted with an insecticide and fungicide mixture, and stored cool (but above freezing-point) where there is air circulation (dry), and preferably in the dark.

Gooseberries
These do best on a deep loam rich in organic matter. They are very susceptible to poor drainage. They often show potash deficiency on light sandy soils. Shallow and light soils should be well enriched to improve moisture retention. They are most likely of all fruits to succeed in chalky soil.

The Care of Gooseberries
The most usual way of growing a gooseberry is as a bush. The lowest branches should not be too low, however, or they may soon droop to the ground. ('Leveller' and 'Careless' are notable offenders in this respect) and if shoot tips take root, a tangle of growth results. To prevent this, start with a leg of at least 6 in. and prune branch leaders to upward-pointing buds.

Pruning Bushes Gooseberries bear their fruit both on wood of the previous year's growth and on spurs arising from older wood. The first few years' pruning should be directed to forming a good open framework of branches: cut branch leaders to half their length and laterals to 3 or 4 buds.

Above: Gooseberry 'Leveller'

Right: Grape Hyacinths

After three years confine winter pruning to removing crossing branches, those congesting the centre and those drooping down to the ground. New upward growing laterals will then have to be selected to replace the old branches and these should be cut back half way to encourage growth. All laterals should be shortened to five leaves in late June.

Pruning could be done in autumn, as soon as the leaves fall, but it is often deferred until spring to discourage the birds which, in some districts, can do much damage pecking out the growth buds.

Protection against birds can, of course, be provided during the winter and in some areas may prove essential. It is not normally necessary to protect the berries while they are unripe but once ripening begins it is.

Trained Forms Gooseberries can be trained as standards as well as espaliers, fans or single or double cordons.

In pruning cordons cut back in winter the new growth of the vertical leader by a third (but never leaving an extension of more than 10 in.). In the second half of June cut back laterals to four leaves and in winter shorten these laterals to two or three buds.

Feeding Give an annual early spring dressing of $\frac{1}{2}$ oz. sulphate of potash and super-phosphate, per sq. yd. Then follow this with a liberal mulch of farm-yard manure.

Grape Hyacinth
Muscari (Lily family)
M. armeniacum is the kind most frequently offered for sale. It makes little heads of honey-scented deep blue flowers on 6–8-in. stems, with lots of narrow, grass-like leaves. Varieties are 'Heavenly Blue', deep blue; 'Cantab', paler blue; and a white form, though the white commonly sold is *M. botryoides alba*. *M. armeniacum* makes fine sheets of colour in April–May under deciduous shrubs and small trees and also looks well as an edging plant, but soon spreads. It will also naturalize in short turf. *M. botryoides* makes a good

rock garden plant as it is not so invasive; its heads of little bells are smaller and a paler blue.

M. comosum is not so often seen as its variety *monstrosum*, the feather or tassel hyacinth. This has curious heads of dark violet-blue threads on 12–15-in. stems in May–June.

M. tubergenianum, the so-called 'Oxford and Cambridge' grape hyacinth, has pale and dark blue flowers on the same head. It is best grown on the rock garden where it will flower in March–April.

Plant *M. armeniacum*, *M. botryoides* and *M. tubergenianum* 3 in. deep and the others 4 in. deep in any good soil in a sunny position. They will all grow on limey soil. Split clumps as necessary after flowering.

Greenhouses
Choosing Your Greenhouse
Buying a greenhouse is an investment, not only because it increases the value of your property but because of the all-the-year-round pleasure it will give.

Since there are many kinds of greenhouse available, in various sizes and made of different materials it is important to choose the one that will best suit your needs. This will depend on a number of factors, including the site available, the plants you intend to grow and the price. Price will govern the size, although it is wise to buy the largest house you can afford to begin with.

What can be grown in a greenhouse largely depends on the temperature that can be maintained. At one time, in large private gardens, a range of houses was to be found, starting from the cold house and passing from the cool to the intermediate and hot or stove house. Today few gardeners can afford more than one greenhouse.

Types of Greenhouse
The Cold Greenhouse This is one which is never heated by anything but the sun and a colourful display can be had without any artificial heat. In extra-cold weather, some protection can be given by blinds which can be pulled down or let up at will. Outdoors, many plants are killed by winter dampness but if taken indoors they come through bad weather unscathed.

Where space is scarce the staging can be erected in tiers. Slatted wood is useful in that it allows air to circulate round the pots, helping to avoid atmo-

Above: Plants in a cool greenhouse

*Right: Types of greenhouse
1: span type and 2: lean-to
model both with low wooden
walls. 3: a span type greenhouse
with glass to the ground. 4: a
modern 'circular' greenhouse
with glass to the ground.
5: a three-quarter span type*

spheric dampness in winter. Unfortunately, it also encourages pots to dry out quickly in summer.

The best plan is to place corrugated or asbestos sheeting over the staging and cover it with fine shingle or stone chips. In summer the shingle can be kept damp to provide humidity, while from late autumn onwards, through winter, it can be allowed to dry.

The Cool Greenhouse   This is one where a minimum night temperature of 40–45°F (4–7°C) can be maintained. This must be controlled, which means adequate ventilation. It is, perhaps, plants in smaller greenhouses that suffer most when air conditioning is wrong, especially if sufficient ventilators have not been provided. Fresh air is important but when the air vents are opened, this naturally lowers the temperature but equally important, it moves the stagnant dark air, leading to the buoyant atmosphere so vital for plant health.

The Intermediate or Warm House A winter night temperature above 48°F (8–9°C) will allow a wider range of exotic plants to be cultivated. Such houses are usually sited where the benefit of all available sun is felt.

It pays to install automatic ventilation which acts according to outside weather conditions and inside temperature. Costing nothing to run, it is easily fitted.

A Hot (or Stove) House This is one where the winter temperature never falls below 60°F (16°C). As it is fairly expensive to run not many amateur gardeners can afford a house of this type. Except for the temperature difference and the fact that a wider range of tender plants, including many orchids, can be grown, the inside arrangements and attention needed, are the same as for the cold greenhouse.

The use of a greenhouse plus a frame means that a kind of shuttle service is operated. Many young plants may be started in the greenhouse early in the year, moved to the frame in summer, and taken back to the greenhouse again in autumn if necessary.

Hedges

There are one or two rules that the hedge planter should learn.

The Site First must be the suitability of the plants used for the site. Most of the usual hedging plants and most of the unusual ones will tolerate a wide range of soil, provided they are well drained. Some are better when lime and chalk are present than others. Near the seaside, plants that will stand the salt-laden gales and protect the choicer plants that they shield are essential: several of these will not stand the harder frosts of inland districts.

When deciding to plant a hedge, apart from considering its position from the point of view of appearance, remember that a hedge has to be cut on two sides and make sure you are going to leave plenty of room on both sides,

not only the one you will be looking at, to give easy access for this clipping.

Hedging plants are like other garden plants: the better their soil conditions the better they grow.

Planting A strip about a yard wide should be marked out where the plants are to grow and should be dug – it is a good idea to work in some compost.

A line should be stretched down the centre and the young trees planted carefully against it. A wiggle in the hedge will take a lot of hiding later.

Except in really wet weather, always keep the young hedge well watered until it is established. The use of lawn mowings as a mulch is a valuable help

Above: A 'Tapestry' hedge made up of Prunus pissardii *'Purple Flash' and* Prunus cerasifera *'Green Glow'*

Left: Lonicera nitida *'Baggesen's Gold'*

to the young trees.

Clipping Then, an important rule about clipping; always trim a hedge so that the bottom is wider than the top, that is, so that it tapers slightly from the base to the apex.

Never cut the leading shoots at the top of the hedge until they have reached the final height that you intend. The top will look untidy for a year or two, but do not worry about that.

The planting distances given below are approximate only; if the plants are a little wider apart, they will probably fill up in due course.

No suggestion is given of the height of the plants you should buy. Tell your nurseryman the purpose for which you will require them and remember that

*The evergreen box (*Buxus sempervirens) *is readily clipped to shape*

small plants will soon catch up the bigger and more expensive ones.

Old Favourites

Hawthorn (*Crataegus oxyacantha*) forms most of the field hedges in this country. The shoots are stout and springy, and it is still unsurpassed for a boundary. It should be planted close, about 1 ft. apart. Winter is the usual time for pruning.

Beech The common beech (*Fagus sylvatica*) is one of the most attractive and decorative of hedging plants. Happy on any kind of soil, including chalk, provided it is well drained, it is a fresh green throughout the late spring and summer. Then in autumn the leaves turn russet colour and hang on until May when the fresh new leaves break and push them off. If the young trees are planted about 1½–2 ft. apart, a good hedge soon results. The best time to clip the hedge is in summer when the leaves are fully unfolded. It can be clipped very hard and close so as to make, if so desired, a very narrow hedge, the growth being so twiggy that it becomes very dense.

To make a vari-coloured beech hedge, seedlings of the copper and purple kinds may be mixed in a random way with the normal form.

Hornbeam Rather similar and particularly good on chalk soils, is hornbeam (*Carpinus betulus*).

Yew The yew (*Taxus baccata*), is another widely used hedging plant. It is seldom used as a purely protective hedge for outer boundaries but more often as an internal, formal division, its sombre green making a fine background for flowers.

Young plants should be set about 2 ft. apart in October or April and watered freely during dry weather in spring. It is particularly important not to cut the leading shoot until it has reached the final required height. The sides should be clipped back hard on a slight slope so that the base of the hedge is broader than the top. Pruning can be done after the spring growth has finished.

Yew can be poisonous to animals, particularly the prunings, which should never be thrown where stock can get at them.

Box Another old favourite for evergreen hedges was box (*Buxus sempervirens*). This is not an ideal material; it is subject to disease and has a wide spreading, greedy root system. This is not the same as the dwarf kind, *B. suffruticosa* used for edging, which must be placed close. The roots of this also rob the beds which it surrounds. Shrubs such as lavender are better.

Some Newer Kinds

The following are of comparatively recent introduction and are also suitable for hedges, particularly those that are informal.

Berberis Several of these prickly shrubs are quite often used for hedging. *B. stenophylla* and *B. thunbergii* are generally recommended. Neither stand pruning and in time become thin at the base.

Cotoneaster Various species are particularly useful as informal, decorative hedges that need no more than trimming to keep them tidy. All carry red or orange berries, eventually enjoyed by birds. *C. simonsii* is a semi-evergreen of close, erect growth which if pruned hard in spring will eventually form a quite rigid hedge some 5 ft. tall. As a contrast the evergreen *C. franchettii* is of close, bushy growth with arching branches which can be lightly pruned to keep it about 7 or 8 ft. The leaves are green above, grey below. Both may be planted about 2 ft. apart.

Euonymus *E. japonica* is an evergreen shrub with glossy leaves, reaching about 10 or 12 ft., which is a valuable and fairly common hedging plant virtually restricted to sea-side gardens where it withstands the salt-laden gales. It is not generally hardy inland. Plant at about 18 in.

Griselinia The large, leathery, evergreen leaves of *G. littoralis* can stand strong winds and salt spray but the shrub is hardy only in mild districts inland. It is often used for hedges, when plants are set about 3 ft. apart. It will grow about 8 ft. tall and needs little pruning. It will grow on chalk.

Lavandula The grey-leaved, fragrant lavender, *L. spica* has for centuries been used as a low hedge reaching 3 ft.

It must have sun, likes lime and should be kept lightly clipped. It will grow by the sea. Plant 18 in. apart.

Lonicera L. nitida, a very small-leaved evergreen honeysuckle (though no one would guess its relationship to the honeysuckle of our hedgerows), is quick growing and suitable for low hedges. It should be planted about 1 ft. apart and cut back hard afterwards. It needs good soil. It may be damaged in severe weather. Prune in summer at fairly frequent intervals.

Herbaceous Borders

No single word or term has yet been accepted to cover garden plants, as distinct from bulbs and shrubs, which flower year after year.

'Herbaceous plants', 'hardy perennials', 'border plants', are all inadequate or inaccurate in some respect. Strictly speaking the word 'herbaceous' denotes the decay of each season's growth, with the plant itself remaining alive, but dormant. Delphiniums, phlox and many others have this habit but several, including iris and kniphofia do not, because they retain winter foliage.

Most perennials are adaptable to ordinary garden conditions, but it would be as much a mistake to plant something which naturally prefers shade or moist soil into a dry open situation as it would the other way round. It would also be a mistake to plant something rank or invasive near something that is by nature of slow or lowly growth.

The main thing is to select plants best suited to the place in which they are to grow. The range of available plants is sufficiently wide for this to be achieved, no matter how small the garden, or unkind the soil, so long as it is not completely hemmed in by tall buildings or overhung by large trees to exclude both light and air, and to compete for the available food and water.

The space between plants in a group, should be less than that between the groups themselves. This is because the plants in a group will usually grow and mass together effectively when in flower. But they will probably differ in form and habit from neighbouring groups, and will need extra space to allow for this as well as to allow for vital light and air to give sturdy growth and for access for maintenance. The

average spacing should be about five plants to the square yard. If, for example, groups are of five plants of a kind, this gives a planting distance of about 16 in. from plant to plant within a group. But the space around the group, up to the outer plants in adjoining groups should be 20 in. Spacing depends on the vigour of the plant; a single plant may occupy a square yard or nine plants of a dwarf, slow-growing plant may occupy the same area.

Do not allow the more robust or rapid spreading kinds to overshadow or encroach on those that expand slowly. Those plants with a similar habit and vigour should be placed near to each other to avoid harmful competition. If you are prepared to plan your own bed or border, it is better not to use a stereotyped plan unless you are quite sure that the plants offered are suitable for the site. Making your own plan is not difficult.

The Herb Garden

Some herbs are propagated from seeds; others from pieces of older plants. Some herbs are permanent (perennial or shrubs), some biennial and some annual. Mint is a perennial, angelica biennial, and summer savory an annual.

Herbs do best in a somewhat sheltered position and in the past, in the gardens of large houses, were invariably bounded by walls or hedges. The site was always a sunny one; when you plan a small herb garden choose a place as warm and sunny as possible. One right out in the open is better than a site where a wall, tree or tall hedge casts shade.

The fortunate gardener starts off with the well-drained kitchen garden sort of soil in which most herbs thrive.

Right: A Summer border

Below: Rosemary flowers

Otherwise both drainage and fertility should be improved to provide the right conditions.

In planning a herb garden, however small or large it may be, reserve one square foot of ground space for each plant. Only when you have grown your own herbs and seen just how little or how much room each plant needs will you know for sure which of them can do with less than a square foot and which needs more.

Herbs vary a great deal in height. Bear this is mind in your planting. Fennel, angelica and lovage are tall and are best positioned to the rear of the bed. They can provide an excellent background to lower, bushier plants such as lavender, bergamot, St. John's wort, lady's maid, old warrior and several of the sages. Near the front of the bed is the correct place for common thyme, lemon thyme, apple mint, white mint, purslane, chives, sorrel and other low growing kinds. The thymes and chives may be planted, if you wish, as a border alongside a garden path adjacent to your herb garden.

The mints never remain where they are planted; if you let them, they will try to take over the whole herb garden. Prevent this by planting them in large flower pots. Sink the pots to their rims in the soil. Cheaper than pots are old pails – plastic or metal. Make some drainage holes in the bottom of pails before planting mint in them.

Most herbs which are to be dried should be cut on a dry and sunny day. Use scissors or secateurs rather than attempt to pick them with your fingers. You want the stems to come clean and not with pieces of root adhering. Gather tips rather than the full stem. Often after you have picked a crop like this side shoots will develop to give you a new harvest later in the summer and autumn.

Hosta
Plantain Lily

These plants have come into their own in recent years, because of their hardiness, adaptability, reliable growth, good foliage and pleasing overall appearance. In any, but parched or starved conditions they can be left for years to develop into solid clumps. They are happiest in cool shade. They vary in height from 8 in. to 4 ft. and can be used in a wide range of places from waterside to woodland condi-

tions, for edging and for a mixed bed or border. *H. crispula*, 3 ft., has handsome leaves edged with creamy-buff and lavender-mauve flowers from June to August. *H. fortunei* and its varieties flower earlier. The species has large pointed blue–green leaves and 2-ft. stems of pale lavender flowers. *H.f. picta* comes through in spring with bright and very attractive variegations which last until flowering at midsummer, before turning green. 'Honeybells' is a green-leaved variety, with 2½-ft. spikes of sweetly scented lavender trumpets. *H. lancifolia* has 20-in. lavender spikes in late summer. *H. rectifolia*, 4 ft., is a splendid freeflowering plant with lavender-mauve spikes. *H. undulata media variegata* has brightly variegated leaves all summer and 12 to 18 in. spikes of deep mauve flowers. *H. ventricosa*, 3 ft., is easy and reliable. It bears deep lavender trumpets freely in July and August and has bluish leaves; in its variety *variegata*, they are deep green and have streaks of yellow which make it one of the most attractive kinds. Hostas are best divided in early spring.

Hyacinths
Lily family

The Roman hyacinths usually have several slender, loosely-packed spikes

Below: Hyacinths

Right: Lace-cap hydrangeas 'Blue Wave' with fertile flowers surrounded by large white bracts

per bulb; the more spectacular, stiff-spiked 'Dutch' ones have the flowers closely packed. Both are very fragrant.

The Dutch hyacinths may be bought 'specially prepared' and these should be planted as soon as available to give flowers in the greenhouse or indoors by late December or early January. They force well.

For indoors they may be grown in water only, in special hyacinth glasses (discard the bulb after flowering); singly in $3\frac{1}{2}$ in. pots, or close packed in larger pots or bowls, with their 'noses' just uncovered. Use bulb fibre for bowls and start these in a cold shed or shaded frame so that they are not drowned by rain; pots may be plunged in a cool place outdoors. Do not bring them into the warmth until the roots are well developed and the shoot is starting to grow (usually from 8–10 weeks). Then keep in full light.

Unprepared bulbs which flower about 3 weeks later may be planted in succession to flower from January to April.

Outdoor hyacinths should be planted in rich soil at least 5 in. deep in October–November. If used for formal bedding they should be replaced each season, but if fed well will make good clumps among shrubs.

The Roman hyacinths, which are white, pink or blue, are sometimes used on rock gardens, but are at their best indoors.

After flowering allow the leaves to die down naturally.

Hydrangea
(Deciduous, medium growing shrub)
All hydrangeas like rich, fairly moist but well-drained soil, and prefer light shade. Though ideal for pots and greenhouse culture, or in tubs, most are quite hardy. In general, blue kinds will only come true to that colour in acid soil or when watered with a special blueing mixture. The pink and red kinds do best on slightly alkaline soil.

In the most popular kinds of cultivated hydrangeas, the 'Hortensia' varieties, only showy infertile flowers are present, built up into globular large heads. There is a wide range of colours and sizes.

In the lace-cap hydrangeas the flower head is flat, with an outer ring of false petals at the centre of which are small florets. One of the best and hardiest is 'Blue Wave' 4 ft. or 5 ft.

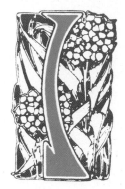

Indoor Plants
House Plants

Conditions indoors are often unsuitable for plants mainly because the atmosphere is very dry. The majority of house plants are evergreens from tropical countries where the atmosphere is damp. A moist atmosphere in the house is uncomfortable but it is possible to create a moist zone around plants, by standing the pot or pots in some container, which will either contain water or which can be kept moist. You can put pebbles in a dish, nearly cover them with water and stand the pot on the pebbles, or you can get rather a deep bowl, plunge the pot in some moisture-retaining material, which can be peat, or sand or moss, and keep this surround always rather moist.

Light Compared to even a rather shady situation outside the light in rooms is not very satisfactory. It is, naturally, at its best on the window-sill and goes down to a near impossible level in corridors and halls. Some plants have evolved to grow in extremely poor light conditions, but it is only in the very densest forests that you will find the dark conditions of parts of our houses. Plants tend to grow towards the light, so if your plant is lit from one window only, turn it slightly every week, so that all parts of the plant will be illuminated in turn.

Leaves and Roots Most plants have two main feeding organs, the leaves and the roots. The leaves can take in plenty of nourishment and syringing them with a foliar feed will have surprising results, but their main function is to make food for the plant. The roots will take up moisture and various chemicals from the soil. Normally neither can subsist without the other, but some plants do dispense with roots to a greater or lesser extent. A very few flowering plants dispense with leaves, but they can only do this by robbing

other plants. Most plants require air, water and soil before they can function.

Air Apart from increasing the humidity of the air, there are other considerations. Draughts are appreciated by plants as little as they are by humans. A draught is a localized stream of cold air, which will attack a portion of the plant only. This will first cause the leaves to drop and may eventually kill the plant, so a very draughty situation should be avoided.

Fumes from various forms of heating are another problem. Paraffin oil heaters are normally fairly innocuous, although a few plants will shed leaves if placed near them, but if something

A sunny room is enlivened by a Ficus benjamina, Monstera deliciosa *and* Philodendron hastatum

goes wrong and the appliance smokes, you may well find many of your house plants dying. The fumes from gas fires used to be harmful to many plants, but the fumes of North Sea gas do not seem to damage plants. Coal fires seem to be harmless and, of course, central heating which maintains a more or less even temperature, is the ideal.

In the open air it is a safe assumption that the temperature will be lower at night than during the daylight hours.

If you are out at work all day, and you do not have central heating, you will not light your fires until you come home, so that you may get the appalling conditions, from the plant's point of view, of a cold day and a hot evening. Many plants are very tolerant and can survive these unnatural conditions, but bear in mind that it is the daytime temperature that is the important figure to watch, as it is during the daylight hours that most of the growth is made. The fact that your room at night may be at a temperature of 70°F (21°C) does not mean that you can grow the plants that require this temperature, if it is liable to fall to 45°F (9°C) at midday. Minimum winter temperatures refer to the daytime readings, and these may fall a few degrees at night without any harm being done, so that you can air the room at night without qualms. During very frosty weather plants that are on the window-sills should be brought further into the room, as it is quite possible for the window panes to be freezing, even though the rest of the room is quite comfortable and frost will certainly damage any house plants on window-sills and may kill them.

Apart from frost many plants from warm climates will survive at temperatures that are lower than they require to make growth. For example, the popular *Philodendron scandens* will go through the winter quite happily with the temperature as low as 45°F (9°C), but it will be in a state of suspended animation. Not until the temperature reaches 60°F (15°C) will it start to make any growth. The recommended winter temperatures for house plants are usually about 10°F (5½°C) below the growth temperature, which means that if they are adhered to the plant will survive perfectly well, but will not be making any growth. The point of this is that growth made during the short daylight hours of winter is usually not very decorative. The stems are liable to become spindly and drawn, while the leaves will be small and a bad colour. Indeed with foliage plants it is usual in the spring to nip out all the growing points and any bad growth that has been made in the winter, so that when the plant does start into growth again, the growth will be well-leaved and the plant will become bushy rather than drawn. However, there are available enclosed glass boxes with their own heating and illumination and in these it

How to provide local humidity for indoor plants. Top: Place pebbles in the base of a bowl; Centre: Cover the pebbles with water and stand the plant pot on the pebbles; Below: Place the pot inside a larger one, filling the space between with dampened peat

is possible to keep tropical plants growing evenly throughout the year.

It is customary to put house plants into three categories: Cool, Intermediate and Warm. The Cool group need a winter temperature of 45–50°F (7–10°C), while a few, notably ivies and fatshedera, will tolerate even lower temperatures. The Intermediate group need winter temperatures around 55°F (13°C), while the Warm group need a temperature around 65–70°F (18–21°C). During the summer they will need at least 10°F (5½°C) more. Few people can manage to maintain any higher temperatures and plants needing them are not discussed here.

Soil Nowadays one has a choice of two sorts of compost, those containing loam and those without loam, known as soilless composts. The most popular compost containing loam is the John Innes Potting compost, usually referred to as J.I.P. This is probably the best compost that one can purchase ready mixed. J.I.P.1 is used for plants in 3-in. pots, J.I.P.2 is used for plants in 5- and 6-in. pots. For larger pots use J.I.P.3.

Good quality loam is hard to come by in large quantities and so the peat-based composts are now being increasingly used. These are mixtures of peat and sand with added chemicals. Peat and sand contain no nutrients so that when the plant has used all the chemicals in the soilless compost it will starve. With plants that are only going to be kept for a single season, for example, *Primula malacoides*, this does not matter; but with plants that are going to be grown on from year to year, it is necessary to start replacing the chemicals as soon as the plant starts to use those already there to avoid all risk of starvation.

Feeding Most house plants make their main growth between the end of March and the middle of September and this is the time to replace the chemicals by some form of feeding. There are various proprietary feeds, all of equal value, but it is necessary to follow the directions as to the amount and frequency of application. As the plant can take up only a limited amount at a time, little and often is better than large quantities at long intervals. Moreover any food not available to the plant is liable to be

Primula malacoides

washed out during subsequent waterings, so it is not only potentially dangerous, but also wasteful to give too much food in any single application. Most of the feeds are applied to the soil dissolved in water and these should not be given when the plant is completely dry, otherwise the chemicals could damage the roots. Feeds are best applied about two days after the normal watering, when the soil will not be completely dry, but equally will not be sodden. It is also possible to apply foliar feeds to the leaves, by syringing the plant with a foliar feed solution. This is one of the best ways of feeding a plant, but it may not be convenient to syringe plants in your rooms. It is, however, usually possible to remove all the plants to your draining board and syringe them there.

Repotting As the plants grow, so do their roots and after a time it is necessary to move the plant to a larger pot. Most plants will want potting on yearly for the first few years.

The usual progression is from a 3-in. pot into a 5-in. pot and thence into a 6-in., 7-in. and finally 8-in., in which pot it will probably remain, as plants in larger pots tend to be very large and unwieldy. Once you reach the 6-in. pot, it will probably suffice to pot on only every other year, so that it will be six years before you reach the 8-in. pot. Potting on should only be done when the plant is in full growth, so that May is usually the best month. If you tip the plant out of its pot (which is best done a day or so after watering) you can see if there are plenty of roots and if these are showing white tips. If the pot appears to be full of roots and these have their white growing tips, the plant is ready for potting on. This is best done when the plant is on the dry side, although it should not be dust dry or the soil may fall away from the roots when you take it out of the pot.

Take the plant out of its pot and lay it on the potting bench, or the draining board. If you are using a loamy compost, put some coarse grit or broken crocks at the base of the new pot; with loamless composts this can be dispensed with. Now place some of the compost in the base of the pot and stand the old pot in the middle to see

Sansevieria trifasciata Laurentii
(back), with a group of
Dracaenas

if you have enough in. In pots up to 3-in. there should be a gap of $\frac{1}{2}$ in. between the soil level and the rim of the pot, while for larger pots the gap should be an inch. If the level is too high, you will not get all the soil moistened when you water; if it is too low, you will get too much water and also the plant will not have all the soil that it could have, so this is a matter worth paying attention to. When you have the right level, fill in around the old soil ball with the new compost, firming it down with your fingers. The new soil you are using should be on the dry side and crumbly, but not dust dry.

Once repotting has been completed, give the plant a good watering, after which it should be allowed to dry out and only watered sparingly for the next week or so. Putting the plant in a warmer situation will encourage the roots to grow more rapidly into the new soil. No feeding is necessary until this new soil has been occupied by fresh roots.

Watering The most essential part in the successful growing of house plants is in the correct use of water and more plants are lost through drowning than through any other cause. When you do water, you should do it properly. Fill the pot to the brim. If you give less it may well not moisten the whole of the soil ball. It does no harm to make sure of this and to turn out a plant a few hours after watering to see if the soil ball has been watered. If it has not, the only thing to do, if the plant is not in a state to be repotted, is to give two applications each time you water.

If you have some method of catching and keeping it, rain water is much to be preferred to tap water, but it is not always possible to obtain this. During the winter, very cold water will lower the temperature of the soil in the pot, perhaps to an excessive degree. Ideally the water should be at the same temperature as your room. You can get this either by mixing some hot water with the cold water, or by storing some water in your room for at least 24 hours before you use it. With most plants the temperature of the water is not very critical, but as far as African violets (saintpaulias), are concerned, if the temperature of the water is lower than 53°F (13°C) you are liable to get unsightly blotches on the leaves. Always, during cold weather particularly, avoid using very cold water, or water that is

more than lukewarm, otherwise you can again damage the roots. Having watered the plant, give it no more water until it has used up all the water you have applied. The smaller the pot, the sooner the soil will dry out, so that plants in 3-in. pots will require rewatering sooner than plants of the same species in 5-in. pots. Plastic pots, not being porous, retain water for longer than clay pots. During spring and summer the plant will absorb water much more rapidly than during the autumn and winter, when growth is almost stationary and all the plant requires to do is to replace any water it may have lost through its leaves. It will lose more in high temperatures than in lower ones, so the room temperature in autumn and winter is also a factor.

There can be no hard and fast rules for watering plants, as, for example, once a week or once a fortnight, but if you inspect your plants daily, you will notice when the soil dries out. Soil at the top of the pot may well be dry while the lower portion is still reasonably moist, so wait for 24 hours after the top soil looks dry and then water. In this way there is little risk of overwatering.

If, when you water, the water runs straight through the pot and out at the bottom, the soil must have become over dry and shrunk. This can usually be cured by firming the soil around the edge of the pot with your thumbs, but if this is not effective fill a bucket with water to the level of the pot and stand the pot in this water and leave it there for 2 or 3 hours, then remove it and firm down around the edge of the pot. Mother-in-law's tongue (*Sansevieria trifasciata laurentii*) is only watered once a month during the winter and this could well be excessively dried out when you want to give more water in the spring, so for this and similar plants the bucket treatment may be necessary.

Leaves wilting is usually a sign of a plant needing water, but it is not a certain sign. If a plant is dying as a result of overwatering, the leaves may well wilt, so that if you see wilting with a wet soil ball, you can be fairly sure that you must let the plant dry out (although your chances of getting it to recover are pretty slim). Also leaves may wilt if they are in burning sunlight. They will immediately recover if placed in the shade or if they are given a light spray with cool water and this phenomenon is, in any case, only temporary; the leaves wilt to prevent excessive loss of water. If the leaves are wilting, inspect the plant and if it is dry, then watering is the answer, but do not water wilting plants unless you have made sure that they are dry.

Cleaning Leaves In towns and industrial districts, the air is liable to be polluted and some attention must be paid to the plant's hygiene. The plant 'breathes' through its leaves and if these get clogged up with dust, the plant will not grow well. It is, therefore, advisable to sponge the leaves once a week. Use a piece of cotton wool and lukewarm water, but sponge the mature leaves only, as the young leaves are soft and could be damaged.

Pest Control Insect pests are uncommon on house plants, but can be prevented from spreading by means of this weekly sponging; even greenfly can be removed in this manner. Aerosol insecticides are available to deal with any serious infection, but these are often poisonous, so they should be kept away from children and the aerosol should not be applied in the house, but in the open air or in an outhouse or garage in inclement weather.

Stopping Many house plants have a stem from which side branches emerge. With such plants, it is usually good policy to remove the growing point, as well as any unsatisfactory winter-made growth in the spring. Stopping will encourage the production of side shoots, so that you have a nice bushy plant as opposed to a rather thin lanky one. However, there is no use in stopping a plant unless it is well-rooted and making good growth. If it is not, all you will do is get another growing point to replace the one you have removed and the plant will not bush out. With some vigorous plants, such as tradescantias, it may be necessary to stop two or three times during the growing season and sometimes with such plants not only the main growing point is removed, but the side shoots are also stopped when they have elongated sufficiently. Further details about whether or not to stop will be found under the descriptions of individual plants.

Propagation Some house plants can be easily propagated from tip cuttings in the home without any elaborate paraphernalia. For these you take a piece of the plant with the growing tip and some 2–4 in. of stem, depending on the ultimate size of the plant; low growing plants will not have much stem. Now make a clean cut with a razor blade at the lowest leaf joint. Then remove most of the lower leaves, if your cutting is very leafy, leaving only about a third of the leaves. Fill a small pot either with a ready purchased cutting compost (the soilless ones are very satisfactory) or with a mixture of equal parts (by bulk) of peat and sharp sand, and then insert your cuttings to a depth of about $\frac{1}{2}$ in. Water them in and then enclose the pot in a polythene bag (or invert a large glass jar over the pot). The pot should be stood in a shady situation.

The best time to take cuttings is between mid-May and mid-August and the worst possible time is during the winter when rooting will probably not take place at all. Rooting usually takes place between 3 and 6 weeks after taking the cuttings. If you see new leaves being produced, that is a fairly reliable sign of rooting. Another method is to give a very gentle tug to the cutting; if there is some resistance it is probably rooted, but if it just comes out, it must be reinserted and you must wait longer. Once the cuttings are

A conservatory can be simple or elaborate – from glass shelves across a large window to a partially or completely enclosed porch or balcony

Pelargoniums in a window box

rooted, remove the polythene bag or glass jar, and wait a week. Then knock the potful of cuttings out and pot each one up separately, taking care to damage the roots as little as possible. The newly potted-up plants should be put in a warm place for a week or so and then they can be moved to their permanent situation. One or two plants require special treatment, but this is noted below. Some plants will root faster if the pot is placed in the airing cupboard; cuttings do not seem to mind being in darkness while they are making their roots, but once these are made, the cuttings must be brought out into the light and it is probably better to be patient and keep the pots outside.

House Plants Described
Flowering Plants   There are two flowering plants that will do well under the coolest conditions; these are the geranium *(Pelargonium × hortorum)* a particularly popular variety of which is *P. peltatum* (ivy-leaved geranium) and the fuchsia. Fuchsias of pyramid shape look best indoors.

When grown in the house, pelargoniums should be given as much light as possible, preferably on sunny window-sills. Fuchsias like a well-lit, but not sunny situation and will do perfectly well in the centre of the room. They do not mind shade, provided it is not dark shade.

Busy Lizzie *(Impatiens walleriana)* is a popular flowering plant for rooms, but the purple-leaved *Impatiens petersiana* is better. This is like the old busy Lizzie with its scarlet flowers, which

are produced freely in quite shady situations as well as in well-lit ones, but its dark purple leaves make it attractive even when it is not in flower. Cuttings root so easily that all you have to do is to put them in water and roots will soon start to appear. As the season advances the plants tend to become leggy and the lower leaves drop off, so it is best to replace the plants at frequent intervals. If you do not want to start them in water, you can insert them in the usual cutting mixture, but there is no need to cover this with a polythene bag. It is practically impossible to overwater these plants during the spring and summer, and they require plenty during this period. During the autumn and winter they must be kept just moist and they also require to be fairly warm, preferably around 55°F (13°C), although they will survive

at 50°F (10°C). Stopping may encourage bushy growth, but they seem to do quite well without any encouragement. Since the plants are normally only kept for the one season, soilless composts will be quite satisfactory without additional feeding.

One of the best and most easily grown house plants for continuous flowering is the Barbados heather *(Cuphea hyssopifolia)*. This makes a small, twiggy shrub with every twig covered with leaves, about 1 in. long and $\frac{1}{4}$ in. across. From the axils of these leaves emerge innumerable small purple trumpet-shaped flowers. Flowering starts in April or early May and will go on non-stop until November. During the winter a temperature of 55°F (13°C) is advisable, but if it falls below this occasionally, no harm seems to occur. Tip cuttings, which should not be too soft, root rather slowly in warm conditions, which probably means that you cannot take them until June, unless you have a heated propagating case. The plant should be grown on year after year, but when it is three years old it may be rather too large (although in this case you can prune harder) so occasional propagation is a good thing. At the end of March it should be pruned, shortening all the main shoots by about 2 in., but otherwise no stopping is necessary. The plant should be potted on every year in April and regular feeding from June until September will encourage more growth and flowers. It likes a well-lit situation and does not mind

*Pelargoniums and petunias
growing on a balcony railing*

some direct sunlight, so long as it is not excessively burning. During the winter it should, of course, receive as much light as possible.

The shrimp plant *(Beloperone guttata)* is another small soft-leaved twiggy shrub, with heads of flowers at the ends of the branches. The flowers are concealed in the bracts, which form a shape like the body of a prawn and are either maroon-purple or, in the form known as 'lutea', a pale yellow. These are produced fairly continuously throughout the summer and autumn and, if conditions are warm enough, well into the winter.

During the winter the temperature should be 55°F (13°C) and the plant should be given as much light as possible. In the spring all the main growths should be cut back by a third, or the plant will tend to become rather leggy with a bare base. Once in a 5-in. pot it can remain there for two years, provided it is fed between mid-May and mid-September and the same period when it is potted on into a 6-in. pot. The plant should be kept moist all the year round, although it will require far less water during the winter months and it should be in a well-lit position that does not receive much direct sunlight.

If you keep your house very warm in the winter, beloperones may produce a lot of weak spindly growth, which looks unhealthy. Remove this in early spring. The plants should be fairly warm, around 65°F (18°C) between the spring pruning and the appearance of the first flowers and higher temperatures will do no harm. Once the flowers have appeared they will persist for longer under cooler conditions, but this sort of temperature adjustment is not very easy in the home and the plant will grow quite happily whatever the temperature is, within reason.

Foliage Plants There is a much larger range of plants with attractive foliage. Many of these plants are variegated. This variegation tends to be more marked in well-lit situations and the most variegated plants need more light than the normal green-leaved forms. On the other hand many green-leaved plants will thrive in shady conditions which would be unsuitable for either flowering or variegated plants, so they have definite advantages. The only plant that will survive in very dark shade is the aspidistra. However, there

Hedera helix 'Little Eva'

are numerous situations where foliage plants will grow happily, although they would be too dark for flowering plants. Foliage plants also have the advantage that they look attractive throughout the year, while even the best flowering plants have some period when they are not flowering, so in many ways the foliage plant gives you better value for your money.

Plants for Cool Conditions
Some plants like cool conditions, with the winter temperature ranging between 45 and 50°F (7–10°C). These plants will not enjoy higher temperatures, although many of those in the next group, needing a temperature of 55–60°F (13–16°C) will survive a winter either with lower or higher temperatures, without any ill effects. Plants that thrive in cool conditions will not necessarily like to be warm in winter, so choose other plants for your warm rooms.

The most notable cool-growing plants are the various ivies, the tradescantias, eucalyptus, chlorophytum, *Ficus pumila* and *Araucaria excelsa*.

The ivies are either small-leaved variants of the common ivy, *Hedera helix*, or of the larger leaved Irish ivy, *H. hibernica*, or of the large-leaved vigorous ivy, *H. canariensis*.

Both *H. hibernica* and *H. canariensis* are climbing plants and do best if they are trained up a stake or on trellis work. There are two forms of *H. canariensis* generally available, of which the most popular is the one with variegated leaves, with a wide silver margin and a dark green centre. The other, 'Golden Leaf', has bright glossy green leaves with a yellowish patch in the centre. Although from the Canary Islands, these plants are quite hardy out of doors. They do not make their best impression until they are quite large. On

the other hand many of the forms of the common ivy are satisfactory as small plants. They can be divided into two main sections, those that are self-branching and tend to make erect little bushy plants and those that are either trailers or climbers. The latter either have to be trained up some support or put in a hanging container, which may well look effective, but is a nuisance to water. The self-branching ivies will branch without any stopping, while the trailing forms require to be stopped in order to produce side shoots and will only do this if they are quite sizeable plants: smaller plants will just replace the original growing points and then grow on.

Among the self-branching ivies are 'Pittsburg', 'Chicago', 'Minima', 'Minigreen' and 'Green Ripple' with plain green leaves, while among those variegated with silver are the 'Variegated Chicago', 'Little Diamond', 'Heisse' and 'Goldchild', which is more cream than silver. Among the trailers some good plants are 'Glacier', 'Eva' (sometimes called 'Little Eva'), and 'Maculata'. An unusual plant is 'Jubilee' also known as 'Golden Heart'. This has the centre of the leaf a deep yellow with a dark green margin. Unlike the other ivies it needs as much light as possible and has the disconcerting habit of making a lot of new stem without any leaves; however patience is all that is required as eventually the leaves form. The other ivies will grow happily in quite shaded conditions, although the variegated forms do better in well-lit situations. During the winter you may get some unvariegated leaves coming at the end of the branches. These should be removed at the beginning of March. Ivies should be kept on the dry side at all times.

The so-called German ivy is in reality a climbing groundsel *(Senecio macroglossus variegata)*. It has roughly triangular leaves of dark green and cream and is one of the few house plants that do not require sponging as the leaves are covered with a waxy secretion. It is a vigorous climber that will need frequent stopping and it is a greedy plant, needing ample feeding.

The tradescantias and zebrinas are trailing plants with variegated leaves about 1½ in. long and ¾ in. across. Some of the variegated leaves of tra-

The flowering Shrimp Plant

descantias are liable to revert to green and any green shoot should be removed as detected, as otherwise they will grow so much faster than the variegated portions that they will eventually swamp the plant. This danger does not apply to the tradescantia known as 'Quicksilver', nor to the zebrinas. Too deep a shade may suppress the variegation, otherwise they will thrive in any situation. Trails will root if placed in water and can be put several to a pot and watered in to make new potfuls. The plants soon become rather leggy and are best replaced every one or two years. You must make a hole in which to insert your cutting (which should be about 2 in. long) as they are rather brittle and might break if you just pushed them in. The compost must be kept fairly moist until the cuttings have rooted, which takes about a fortnight. Tradescantias like plenty of water, but if kept dry the leaves will come small but quite well-coloured. Side shoots appear whether you stop the plants or no, but they will appear sooner if you stop the main growths.

The eucalyptus most commonly grown as a house plant is *E. cinerea*, which could eventually make a small tree. It is very attractive with its white branches and blue-green leaves, which are nearly circular in young plants and lance-shaped when adult. To keep the plant within reasonable bounds it must be pruned hard every spring and the leading shoots that emerge at the top of the plant must then be stopped, otherwise they will continue to grow and no lower growths will be formed. The plant should have a well-lit situation and be kept reasonably cool during the winter. Once in a 6-in. pot, it is advisable to keep it there, as otherwise the resultant plant might become too unwieldy. This entails regular feeding.

Chlorophytum comosum variegatum is sometimes known as the spider plant. It throws up a clump of grassy leaves, which are nearly a foot long, but which reflex to give a fountain-like effect. They are either cream-coloured with a thin green margin or else they have green margins and a cream centre. The small white flowers are often replaced with a tuft of leaves and if this is pinned down into a pot it will soon take root and the stem can then be severed, giving you a fresh plant. Keep these young plants somewhat on the dry side until they are well rooted, but well-rooted

plants can take plenty of water during their growing season, although they are kept fairly dry from October until March. Small plants look rather grassy, but they grow rapidly and large plants are very impressive. They should be put into 5-in. pots as soon as possible and then potted on every other year.

Ficus pumila is a low creeping plant, producing aerial roots like an ivy and it can be trained up walls in the same way. The leaves are small, about 1 in. long and ½ in. across, heart-shaped,

Left: Trailing plants look their best in a hanging basket

Below: Chlorophytum and Cissus antarctica

and they completely cover the thin wiry stems. This plant thrives in shade and must never be exposed to bright sunlight and similarly it must never be allowed to dry out completely, otherwise the leaves will shrivel and drop off. Over-watering is possible, particularly during the winter, but some moisture is essential even during this period. In mild parts of the country it will grow outside on a north-facing wall, so it has no objection to quite low temperatures.

Araucaria excelsa, the Norfolk Island pine is in nature a very large tree, but it is very slow-growing as a house plant. It makes a perfectly symmetrical pyramid, with a central stem, from which, after every year's growth, four branches radiate horizontally from the

central stem and, in their turn, produce symmetrical side shoots, which are produced in opposite pairs all along these side branches. All these main and side branches are densely clothed with bright green needles. The plant must be rotated at regular intervals, so as to preserve its symmetry. The plant should never be pruned nor stopped and once in a 5-in. pot needs potting on every two or three years, and should be fed during the intervening period. The plant can be stood outside during the summer in a somewhat shaded situation. The plant must not dry out at any time, but on the other hand it does not require much water at any period, although more will be required when the new growths are elongating.

Other house plants that will thrive under cool conditions are two vine-like climbers, *Cissus antarctica*, the kangaroo vine, and *Rhoicissus rhomboidea*, while an attractive trailing plant is *Plectranthus oertendahlii*, with leaves that have the principal veins picked out in silver.

Plants for Intermediate Temperatures
With a constant winter temperature of from 55 to 60°F (13–16°C), the choice is very much wider and many more colourful specimens may be grown. Perhaps the most gorgeous of all are the plants known in the U.S.A. as Ti trees, *Cordyline terminalis*. These are small palm-like plants with leaves up to a foot in length and 4 in. across. They first unfurl with the most brilliant

colours in cerise, pink, or cream and pink and which gradually age to a purplish brown or a medium green with a red margin, but practically any combination of red, pink, cream and green can be found in the various cultivars. Since they grow more or less continuously, the appearance of the plant is constantly changing. Unfortunately, these gorgeous colours do not appear until the plant has been growing some three years, so that they are not cheap to purchase. They are greedy feeders requiring a rich soil mixture and ample feeding. They should be potted on every two years. They must have a well-lit situation, but not in direct sunlight for too long and they require ample water, but should not be over-

watered. Since the leaves are more brightly coloured than a good many flowers, it can be appreciated that this is a fairly striking plant. It is never stopped.

The croton, *Codiaeum variegatum*, is equally colourful, but not quite so easy as it is very sensitive to any fall or violent fluctuations in temperature, which can also have bad results. If the temperature can be kept constant, the plant will thrive. The leaves vary in shape from nearly circular to almost grass-like and are in various combinations of brilliant colours. This can be kept somewhat on the dry side during the winter, but will take plenty of water during the summer. The plant contains a milky juice, which spurts

Above: Philodendron '*Burgundy*' grows rather slowly as a house plant

Left: The bright-leaved croton, Codiaeum variegatum

out whenever it is damaged. Therefore it should be handled with great care and should never be stopped. It requires ample light at all times and has no objection to direct sunlight. It is by no means one of the easiest of house plants, but it is very showy. Potting on should take place every other year.

Very much easier are the rex begonias. These have roughly triangular leaves, which may be fairly regular or which may have very jagged edges, and these leaves are gorgeously coloured in varying shades; some are deep or rosy purple, others varying shades of green and silver; the choice is very large. They have no objection to shady conditions and will still keep their gorgeous

colours in such situations. Begonias have very fine roots and are usually grown in a mixture composed mainly of leafmould and sand, with only a little loam so that soilless mixtures will prove very satisfactory. They must not dry out at any time, but they do not require too much water either and should be watered regularly. Rex begonias spread outwards rather than upwards and they can be divided, if the plant is getting too large. The plants should be fed during the summer, but rather sparingly. The 'Iron Cross' begonia *(B. masoniana)* needs rather warmer conditions than the rex group and has bright green leaves with a maroon 'Iron Cross' in the centre.

The zebra plant, *Aphelandra squarrosa louisae*, has an upright stem from which spring pairs of leaves, which may be 9 in. long and half as wide. These are a dark green, with the main veins picked out in bold ivory stripes. The original plants produced pyramidal heads of yellow flowers, but the later forms, known as 'Brockfield' and 'Dania' flower very rarely. The plant needs repotting yearly and needs ample water during the summer and a certain amount in the winter. Side shoots can be detached and rooted in the summer, but a temperature of at least 65°F (18°C) is necessary and preferably somewhat higher. These plants need a reasonable amount of light, but will grow in partly shaded conditions quite satisfactorily.

The various ficus are not particularly colourful, but they are impressive. The most popular is the indiarubber tree, *F. elastica*, which is offered either as var. *decora*, which has the immature leaf covered with a red sheath, or as var. *robusta*, which has very large leaves, somewhat rounder than those of *decora*. There are also some handsome variegated forms known as 'Schryvereana' and 'Variegata', with their leaves blotched with cream, light and dark green, which are somewhat more decorative. The indiarubber plant can eventually make an enormous tree, so it is kept to reasonable dimensions by keeping it in a small pot, 5 or 6 in. in diameter, and feeding it during the summer to get the leaves a good size, but not to encourage much stem elongation. Their large leathery leaves must be sponged regularly on both surfaces to keep them glossy and to stop any possible infection with scale insect. They

can be kept fairly dry in the winter and watered normally during the summer, when they will much appreciate the leaves being syringed during very hot spells. They will grow equally well in shade or sun, although they should be in the shade when the new leaves are unfurling, otherwise these will not be a good size. Ordinarily you do not stop at all, but if the plant gets too tall, it can be cut back in spring, when it will break again from lower down. This is a messy job as the plants are full of milky latex (from which rubber can be obtained) and this will gush out and stain the plant. The cut surface should be sprinkled with powdered charcoal immediately to stop excessive bleeding. *Ficus benjamina* is another member of this genus, which makes a branching, thickly-leaved tree with long narrow leaves giving something of the effect of a weeping willow. Some of these leaves will be shed in the winter whatever you do, as it is their natural habit, but many more will be produced in the following spring and summer. This needs a well-lit but shady position and will take rather more water than *F. elastica*.

There are many philodendrons used as house plants; most of them are climbers, producing aerial roots, but one striking plant *P. bipinnatifidum*, does not climb, but forms a rosette of long-stemmed very jagged leaves, which get larger as the plant grows and can end up a yard across. The leaves also get more jagged as the plant matures; the first leaves are heart-shaped. As the larger plants are handsomer, they are potted on yearly until they are in a 7- or 8-in. pot, in which they can then stay, being fed regularly each season. With these larger sized plants clay pots are better than the plastic ones, that are so light that a large plant makes them top heavy. This plant is never stopped. On the other hand the climbing species are stopped from time to time, although not necessarily every year. These climbers all require shady conditions, although these should not be too dark, whereas *P. bipinnatifidum* will grow either in shade or in full light, although the leaves seem to be larger in the shade. Ideally the climbing forms should have a very damp atmosphere from which their aerial roots can obtain nourishment, but they are often tolerant of quite dry conditions. They are sometimes trained on blocks of cork bark, to which the roots adhere and which is quite easy to moisten. The most attractive, but a delicate, rather difficult plant is *P. melanochryson*, with heart-shaped, dark green, iridescent leaves, 5 or 6 in. long. Much easier are the popular *P. scandens*, with green heart-shaped leaves, and two very similar species, *P. hastatum* and a plant *P.* 'Tuxla', both of which have spear-shaped leaves about 7 in. long and 4 in. wide. They are a shining dark green, with some coppery sheen in the young leaves. These latter are fairly slow growers, whereas *P. scandens* is quite fast and benefits from a yearly stopping. If it becomes too tall you can bend the flexible main stem right over and tie it in at the base of the plant, whence it will start to climb anew. A plant needing similar treatment to the climbing philodendrons is *Monstera deliciosa borsigiana*. This has large serrated leaves, which are perforated with holes, giving a very exotic outline. In dark shade these perforations will not develop. It is best trained upright and the aerial roots carefully guided down into the soil in the pot. Stopping is not recommended unless the plant is getting too large, as it is slow to break again. Similar to *P. scandens*, but with gold variegated leaves is *Scindapsus aureus*, which needs more light than the philodendrons and requires a yearly stopping.

Aralia (Dizygotheca) elegantissima makes a slow growing shrub with leaves like those of a horse-chestnut in shape, but the leaflets are extremely thin in young plants, becoming slightly wider as the plant ages. They are coppery red when they emerge but become very dark maroon, almost black. This may not sound very attractive, but the plant has enormous grace and charm, as much from its elegant habit as from its light, graceful leaves. It requires a well-lit position, but shade from much direct sunlight and the leaves should be syringed frequently during the summer and occasionally during the winter to discourage red spider. On the other hand the soil is always watered somewhat sparingly, particularly in the winter.

Mother-in-law's tongue, *Sansevieria trifasciata laurentii*, makes an upright plant, with stiff, fleshy leaves, which are mottled in light and dark green with a golden margin.

The plant often produces only one group of leaves in a year and this may turn up some way from the rest of the plant. There is a temptation to cut this out to form another plant, but this should only be done the year after it has appeared, as it does not produce any roots the first year and the plantlet will probably die. If, when the section is about 8 in. long, you can find the underground stem from which it rises and cut this half-way through with a knife, this seems to encourage rooting. This plant needs ample light and very little water. In the winter one watering a month is sufficient and even in the summer it should be allowed to dry out thoroughly between waterings. The new leaves are somewhat rolled in to start with and water should not be allowed to lodge in this hollow, otherwise the root could rot. Otherwise they are tough resilient plants, which will put up with almost any conditions and tolerate oil or gas fumes.

Peperomias are low plants, with a very small root system. Some have trailing stems, but the most attractive throw up a tuft of leaves from a central point. The best are probably *P. hederaefolia*, *P. caperata* and *P. sandersii*. *P. hederaefolia* has heart-shaped leaves some $2\frac{1}{2}$ in. long and 2 in. across, which have a quilted effect from the undulating surface. They are pale grey with olive green main veins. In the autumn it produces flowers that look like white mouse tails. If a leaf is removed and inserted shallowly in a cutting mixture with the temperature not below 65°F (18°C) a small plant will arise from the base of the leaf. *P caperata* has smaller, corrugated leaves, the peaks appearing greyish, while the valleys have a purple tinge. The flowers are pure white. It is propagated the same way as *P. hederaefolia*, but the stalk can be inserted a little deeper. Both these plants like shady conditions and never a great deal of water around the roots, although they revel in a moist atmosphere. The rugby football plant, *P. sandersii*, is the most handsome of all the peperomias, but is not very easy, requiring a winter temperature of 60°F (16°C) and great care in its placing as it is very sensitive to even mild draughts. The striking leaves, shaped like a rugby football, are silver with green zones around the main veins. Keep the plant as dry as possible in the winter; the leaves can flag before you need to water as they recover quickly.

The calatheas and marantas all have very attractive leaves. They must have moist, shady conditions and the plants need ample feeding during the summer. They will probably need potting on yearly. If plants get very large, they can be divided. Although they will pass the winter happily at the temperatures recommended, they need about 10°F ($5\frac{1}{2}$°C) more during the summer to make proper growth. Direct sunlight can shrivel the leaves, so should be avoided. The plants are sometimes known as prayer plants, as they raise their leaves at night. *Calathea insignis* has elongated oval leaves, 4–9 in. long; they are yellowish-green darkening towards the leaf margin and with dark green blotches along the midrib, while the underside of the leaf is a deep claret colour. *C. mackoyana* is very striking with rounder leaves, about 6 in. long and 4 in. across. The main portion of the leaf is silvery in colour with dark green blotches, underside rosy purple, so that the plant has a rosy glow. *Maranta leuconeura* is a variable plant, rather lower than the calatheas, its leaves usually about 4 in. long and $2\frac{1}{2}$ in. across. The var. *massangeana* has leaves of soft green with the veins picked out in white to give a herringbone effect, while the var. *kerchoveana* has leaves that when young are emerald green with blotches between the veins, while in the older leaves the colours are dark green and maroon. The var. *erythrophylla (tricolor)* has larger, very dark green leaves, the main veins bright red, with yellowish-green blotches between them.

Irises
Of the large and varied family of irises cultivated today, the bearded iris of the *germanica* type is the one most commonly grown. Its poise and elegance and its sword-like leaves that are excellent contrast for the soft foliage of other plants, and its wide range of colourings, make it a perfect gap-filler when tulips are over and border plants not yet at their best.

Colours These range from snowy white through cream to shell pink and apricot, from butter yellow to flax blue, from deep sapphire to ruby red and purple. There are also browns, tans and near blacks as well as bicolours, and

Aphelandra squarrosa
Louisae

the plicatas (a hybrid group) have markings of another colour etched like veins on a paler ground. The upstanding portion of the flower, known as the 'standard' and the drooping tongue-like petal, known as the 'fall' are often different again, so that every conceivable combination of colour exists somewhere in a named cultivar.

Heights The plants vary in height, from dwarfs a few inches high, through the intermediate irises, 16–24-in., to 4-ft. tall kinds. Dwarf bearded irises, forms of *I. pumila* or of *I. chamaeiris* and of many beautiful hybrids, can be used with great effect on rock gardens, in pockets in paving, on dry walls or in sinks and troughs. Their flowers, on stalks a few inches high, resemble the tall flags. They flower during late March and April. They are vigorous and need re-vitalizing by division and re-planting every year or two.

Intermediate Irises These, the result of crossing the dwarfs and the tall kinds, increase quickly and are less susceptible to rhizome-rot than the tall irises. Named cultivars come in a wide variety of colours. Though tall flags are better planted apart from other perennials which prevent the sun from reaching and baking their rhizomes, the intermediate irises are happy at the front of the border. Flowering in May, they prolong the season. They are rarely more than 2 ft. tall.

Tall Bearded Irises The tall bearded irises flower in late May and June. Though the blooms are individually short-lived, a succession of flower-buds ensures weeks of colour. The modern kinds branch out, the better to display their numerous flowers.

Requirements Bearded irises are the most good-natured of hardy plants, provided their modest requirements are met. These are: (1) Proper preparation of the ground before planting. (2) A sunny site. (3) A well-drained soil containing lime, which should be deeply dug, and some humus-forming material incorporated before planting (on no account use animal manure).

Planting Always plant shallowly but firmly, barely covering the rhizome so that the sun can bake it. Artificial fertilizers are not necessary if the soil is fertile; excess of nitrogen leads to lush leaf growth and loss of flower. Plants must be hand-weeded, since hoeing can damage the rhizomes. Flower-stems should be removed as close to the ground as possible.

The best time for planting or dividing is soon after the flowers are finished, when congested clumps should be split up and only the young vigorous fans, each with a rhizome and strong roots, replanted. Space the tall irises 2 ft. apart; the dwarfs and intermediate kinds should be planted more closely.

Bulbous Irises Dwarf bulbous irises provide some of the most striking splashes of colour in the winter garden. *I. danfordiae,* canary yellow, and *I. histrio aintabensis*, blue, flower during January and look well planted together. The brilliant blue *I. histrioides* 'Major', with flowers 4 in. across on short stems, flowers before the leaves appear. The bulbs of these tend to split up into tiny bulblets so that it is best to renew annually, potting on the little offsets until they reach flowering size. In February and March flower the sweetly scented, violet-purple *I. reticulata* and its cultivars, pale blue 'Cantab', reddish-purple 'J. S. Dijt' and dark blue 'Royal Blue'.

The Spanish, Dutch and English irises make good clumps in the border. The Dutch, at 2 ft., flower in May and June. The colours are white, yellow, mauve and blue. They are followed by the Spanish irises, *I. xiphium*, in a similar colour range. Both are excellent cut flowers. Bulbs are so cheap that it is worth planting annually, though many will flower each year in a dry soil. The English irises, *I. xiphioides* flower in June and July.

Kitchen Garden

Intercropping

This is of great use in the small kitchen garden. A quick-to-grow and mature vegetable is grown between two rows of a slower-growing vegetable. A good example is radish sown between two rows of peas. Two somewhat slower-growing vegetables may be grown alongside each other. Thus lettuces may be grown in the vacant spaces left between two rows of peas. A later-to-mature vegetable may be planted in between or alongside rows of another vegetable which will shortly be harvested.

Examples Cabbage plants set out among lettuces about to be cut for use; Brussels sprouts set out alongside rows of dwarf French beans.

Mulching

Mulches are soil covers. Their use saves time in watering and weeding. All mulches are laid down when the soil is moist. They prevent a loss of soil moisture by evaporation. They also smother weed seedlings and usually inhibit the growth of more weeds. Most mulches disintegrate slowly and improve the garden soil. One only does not. This is black polythene sheeting.

Garden compost acts as a plant food as well as a mulch. The food is immediately available to plants mulched with compost. It may itself contain weed seeds. Well-rotted farmyard manure is excellent as a mulch for cucumbers, but must not be used as freely as garden compost around most vegetables. Granulated sedge peat contains little plant food but is the neatest mulching material. Lawn mowings are the most commonly used mulching material, but can attract slugs. Autumn leaves should be partially rotted before being applied. Several sheets of newspaper make a useful but unsightly mulch. It is best covered with a little straw. Straw should not be used around seedlings

because loose straw may blow over and on to them causing damage. Well-rotted or raw sawdust may be used only if the garden soil is highly fertile. Sawdust robs a soil of some nitrogen during decomposition. Wood shavings are liable to blow around at first. Use them only on very fertile soil. They are rather unattractive to the eye. Black polythene sheeting is ugly when laid in position but is camouflaged by rapidly growing vegetables.

Rotation

The main aim of rotating crops is to prevent a build-up of pests and diseases. If cabbages and their kin are grown regularly in the same patch of ground

Above: A well-planned kitchen garden

Below: Intercropping: French beans between celery

Examples of Successional Cropping

Vegetable	Sown or planted	Ground cleared	Sown or planted
Broad beans Peas (first early) Lettuce Spring cabbage	Late summer and autumn	June	Winter cabbage Broccoli
Broad beans Peas (first early) Lettuce Potatoes (first early)	March or April	July	French beans Beetroot Carrots Lettuce Winter radish
Potatoes (second early and maincrop)	March or April	September	Spring cabbage

there is the likelihood of the soil becoming cabbage-sick and infected with club root disease. Should onions be grown often in the same bed an outbreak of onion white rot may occur making the whole garden unfit for onion growing for several years. Where potatoes are frequently grown in the same patch or very near to it a build up of keeled slugs may be expected. A secondary reason for crop rotation has more bearing on a less fertile rather than a highly fertile soil. The theory is that because all vegetables do not utilize the same amounts of plant food in the soil it pays to rotate crops each season. The tomato is noted for its great need of potash and lettuce plants need a lot of nitrogen. By rotating beans and peas in the garden the soil in which they grow is enriched with nitrogen.

For the medium-sized garden, the following three-year rotation is suggested:

First Season Potatoes. Soil dressed with manure or garden compost in autumn, winter or early spring.

Second Season Cabbages and their kin. Soil limed if necessary in winter or early spring. Where available apply manure or garden compost later. Alternatively, apply manure during late autumn or winter when digging the garden. Apply lime where necessary in early spring.

Third Season Other vegetables. No manure or garden compost need be applied for most other vegetables apart from such greedy feeders as cucumbers, marrows and sweet corn.

In a larger garden the rotation may be based on a four-year plan. For this the garden is divided into four sections with planning as follows: *Section A:* potatoes. *Section B:* cabbages and their kin. *Section C:* peas and beans. *Section D:* root crops and other vegetables.

For the second season section A is used for root crops and other vegetables, potatoes are grown in section B, cabbages and their kin in section C, and peas and beans in section D. After the fourth season the rotation is complete and section A is used again for the potato crop.

Successional Cropping

This term covers two different aspects of vegetable growing. Successional sowings of the quick growing radish and fairly quick growing lettuce are made on and off between April and August. Successional planting means that no ground is left vacant throughout the summer. As soon as one crop has been harvested, the soil is prepared at once for a follow-on crop.

Certain vegetables have varieties which are earlier to mature than other varieties. The good gardener chooses, if he knows where there will be available garden space for them, early and later varieties. There is then a succession of the same vegetable for use over a longer period than there would be were only either an early or a later variety grown.

In addition to choosing early and late varieties a greenhouse, an unheated garden frame or a set of cloches can be put to use to extend the season itself. This leads to earlier than usual spring and summer vegetables and a greater choice of fresh vegetables from the garden in late autumn.

The permanent bed of the kitchen garden can be devoted to perennial vegetables such as asparagus if space permits, to a variety of herbs and aromatics – which will have the two edged advantage of perfuming the air as well as being useful in many cooking experiments – and of course to fruit bushes such as gooseberries.

Laburnum
Pea Family
This well-known tree is often called golden rain. It flourishes under all but the most extreme conditions, and is grown for its small, golden pea-shaped flowers which hang from its branches in long chains during May and June. It can be grown as a bush or a standard and needs only the minimum of pruning to shape it. By far the best kind for gardens is the hybrid *L. vossii*, with very long trails of flowers.

Lawns
For new lawns, grass seed is best sown

Laburnums can produce a beautiful archway effect

during September. Clean, weed-free soil and the application of a pre-seeding general fertilizer ten days or so before sowing are advisable; choose a day when the soil is moist and rain is likely to follow, make sure there is a good tilth, and sow the seed evenly. Patchy sowing leads to trouble with damping off disease

Bald parts of established lawns should be scratched up to provide some sort of seedbed and sown with a seed mixture which matches the grasses already present. Breaking edges can be remedied by cutting the turf so that a piece a foot wide and of a convenient length is removed, to include the bad edge, turned round so that the edge is inside, and the turf replaced, filling in the gap now inside the lawn with compost and grass seed.

Brushing, raking with a wire rake, and spiking all help to improve the penetration of air to the turf surface and the soil beneath. The mat of dead vegetation which is likely to form during summer is removed and so, too, are pests which may have been hiding in it, and fungus diseases which can damage the grass.

Lawn Mowers

One of the most useful pieces of equipment is a lawn-mower. The range of machines is considerable and the choice will be conditioned by the area and type of grass which has to be cut. For the average lawn, a 12–14 in. cylinder mower is suitable, especially where a good close cut is desired. The rotary mower will cut reasonably rough, tough and tall grass as well as the normal domestic lawn, but it will give a close cut. For complete ease of starting the electric mower or the battery-powered types should be selected. The former are available in light, easy to manoeuvre designs or in larger and heavier forms for larger grass-cutting requirements. The battery-powered mowers are heavy but are still ideal for the woman gardener, provided the machine has not to be negotiated over steps or other difficult places. Battery mowers are easy to re-charge as they are supplied with a special charger.

Grass-collection is a point worth considering when the rotary mowers are being looked at. Some of the cheaper models do not have this facility. Others have a simple yet efficient designed 'solid' box.

Leeks

Sow seeds late March/early April, keep down weeds and water well in dry weather. Dig up all the seedlings in late June and replant at once. Use a dibber to make holes 4 in. deep about 8 in. apart in rows 1 ft. apart. Drop a seedling into each hole and pour in a little water. Weed when necessary. Dig leeks for use at any time between November and late April.

For Tree Onion and Welsh Onion see Fifty Vegetables and Salads; Chives see Herbs.

Lettuce

There are three different types of lettuce: cabbage, cos and loose leaf. Cabbage lettuces are divided into two groups: *Butterhead*, e.g. 'Unrivalled', 'May King'; *Crisphead*, e.g. 'Webb's Wonderful', 'Windermere'.

Sowing The sowing times are linked closely with varieties. The table shows when to sow for successional crops.

Sow fairly thickly in 1-in. deep drills, 9 in. apart if all the seedlings are to be dug up and the stronger plants transplanted. If the seedlings are to be thinned to leave strong plants at 1 ft. apart in the row, rows should be 1 ft apart. Sow pelleted seeds 1 in. apart. Keep down weeds and water well in dry weather. Cos makes quicker, tighter hearts if tied loosely with string or raffia just when hearting starts.

Lilac
Syringa

The lilacs provide a wide range of colour in their sweetly scented flowers opening from mid to late May. All pre-

When to sow	Where to sow	When to transplant	Suggested varieties	When to harvest
February/March	Frames or cloches	April under cloches	Unrivalled	May and June
Early April	Cloches or open garden	Late April or early May	Unrivalled	Late June and July
Mid to late April	Open garden	Mid to late May	Webb's Wonderful, Giant Crisphead	July
May	Open garden and where plants are to grow	Late May or early June	Little Gem, Giant White, Cos, Buttercrunch, Continuity	July and August
June/July	Open garden where plants are to grow	Young seedlings may be transplanted	Windermere, Peson, Continuity, Little Gem	August and September
Early August	Open garden and where plants are to grow	Do not transplant	Continuity, Salad Bowl	September and October
August	Open garden. Give cloche protection in early October	Do not transplant	Seaqueen, Emerald, Valdor	November and December
Late August	Open garden	Late September. Give cloche protection in October in colder areas	Imperial Winter, Winter Crop	Late April and May
Mid October	Unheated or slightly heated greenhouse	Thin seedlings. Do not transplant	Kiosk	April

fer sun and good fertile soil, particularly if lime is present, but are tolerant of other conditions. Newly planted bushes should be cut hard back to vigorous buds. When plants become dense and thicket-like, a few stout stems should be cut out down to the base as growth starts. It is worth removing the faded flower spikes for the first year or two.

Single Flowers 'Esther Staley', pink, mid-May; 'Maud Notcutt', white, late May; 'Souvenir de Louis Spath', reddish purple, late May.

Double Flowers 'Mme Antoine Buchner', rosy mauve, late May; 'Mme Lemoine', double white, late May; 'Paul Thirion', rosy red, early June.

Lilium
Lily (Lily family)
Lilies are often sold packed in peat or wood shavings to help retain their moisture and protect them. They should be planted as soon as available, from September to January, except for *L. candidum* and *L. testaceum* which are usually moved 'green', i.e. while still in leaf, after June–July flowering. Any lily can be moved successfully immediately after flowering if care is taken to keep the soil on the roots. Some come dry from Japan or N.W. America and these may not be on sale until soil conditions

Above: Cos lettuces produce crisper leaves and whiter hearts if the plants are tied with soft string or raffia as they develop

Below: A fine branch of lilac. Syringa 'Sensation' has purplish-red white-edged flowers

outside are far from ideal. In this case pot them immediately and plant out later when conditions are correct.

With the exception of *L. candidum* and other European lilies such as *L. martagon* which make roots from the base of the bulbs only, lilies should be planted with their soil at least twice the depth of the bulb above it, thus a 2-in. deep bulb would need a hole 6–7 in. deep. This is because many lilies make roots from the stem in the first few inches of soil, in addition to those below the bulb. Sites for such lilies must be weed free, for hoeing near them is disastrous. Many lilies grow wild in the company of low-growing shrubs, the roots of which help to drain the soil, and others are found on steep slopes where moisture is flowing under the surface for much of the year, but all are on well-drained sites, and if necessary special beds must be made with extra peat and sharp sand to retain moisture but allow free drainage. Beds or even hummocks of such soil which will raise the roots and bulbs above the winter water table may make all the difference between success and failure. Some lilies will tolerate lime and others die if given it. Most lilies like to have their flowering stems in the sun, at least for part of the day, and grow well with a ground cover of low shrubs, or even annuals to protect their roots.

Lily bulbs should be examined to make sure there is no basal rot present, as this will cause the scales to fall away.

Such bulbs should be burnt. The bulbs can be dusted with a fungicide to prevent the spread of the fungal disease which causes death of leaves and even of the whole shoot. Once the plants are growing they can be protected from this disease by spraying with a systemic fungicide. Virus diseases are incurable, but their spread can be checked by spraying plants with a systemic insecticide which kills aphids which spread virus diseases. Some lilies are comparatively tolerant of virus diseases, but grow better without them, and others are killed by them. The easiest way to get virus-free stock is to raise the plants from seed and keep them sprayed. This works for most species but garden hybrids will not come true to form or colour. However, if 'strains' of lilies are bought rather than named varieties these will have been raised from seed, whereas the others will have been propagated from off-sets, bulbils and by rooting scale leaves, and the risk of virus is greater with these.

Most lilies can be grown from seed, in fact *L. formosanum* and *L. philippinense*, white trumpet, cool greenhouse lilies, can be had in flower within a year of sowing the seed. However, many take three or four years and *L. martagon* takes six or seven to reach flowering size. *L. regale* flowers after two or three years.

The garden hybrids are officially classified according to their parents' classification.

Many lilies make first-class pot plants. A suitable compost consists of three parts of fibrous loam, one part each of peat (or leafmould), silver sand and decayed manure. Alternatively, J.I.P.3 is suitable. For forcing, plant bulbs in October and November. Use 6- or 7-in. pots and for stem-rooting varieties, leave space in the pots for top-dressing later. Plunge the pots in peat or sandy soil in the cold frame and bring them into a temperature of 40–50°F (4–10°C) early in the year, gradually raising the heat to 60–70°F (16–21°C). Top-dress when growth is 5 or 6 in. high. Where little heat is available, plant bulbs in February for flowering from May onwards. Good varieties for pots include *L. auratum* and *L. speciosum*, both stem-rooting; and *L. longiflorum*, the white Easter lily.

Left: Lilium candidum

Magnolia

All magnolias do best in moist, slightly acid soils, though many will do well when some lime is present. All prefer sunny, sheltered positions but several are tough and extremely hardy. All have fleshy roots and are best planted just before growth begins in spring, using plenty of peat around the roots and watering well and staking firmly until they are established. The most reliable for a small garden is *M. soulangeana* (deciduous, medium growing shrub). This bears large, white cup-shaped flowers with claret coloured bases, from April to May; a pure white form ('Alba') and one with purplish flowers ('Rubra') are available. All have spreading, stout branching systems. They will flower when 3 ft. or so high and under ideal conditions will become small trees. Little pruning other than to shape the bushes is needed. None likes root disturbance – e.g. the forking of ground underneath them.

M. stellata is the smallest magnolia; it forms a compact shrub with very numerous white many-petalled flowers about 3 in. across in March and April. It is suitable for the smallest garden.

Marrow

Fertile, well-drained soil is necessary for the good growth of these plants as they are greedy feeders.

Sowing Sow seeds the last week of April or the first week of May. In the south of England there is sufficient sun heat in the greenhouse for seed of vegetable marrow and pumpkin to germinate well. In other parts of the country it is an advantage to have some form of heating so that night temperatures do not fall below 50°F (10°C).

Fill 3½-in. pots with the potting compost of your choice. Make sure the compost is moist. Then press two seeds into the compost in each pot. Water lightly, with a fine rose on the watering can. Keep the pots moist but not over-wet. Germination takes about a week. When seedlings are forming the first true (triangular) leaf, pinch off the second, weaker seedling in each pot. Do not pull out this unwanted seedling. If you do, you may disturb the roots of the seedling you wish to retain. From now on until planting time keep the seedlings moist. Growth is very rapid.

Marrow Varieties

Some varieties produce plants which are low, compact bushes, other varieties make long, trailing stems. These varieties are known as 'trailers'. Popular varieties are:

Bush Bush Green; Bush White; Early Gem (F_1); Gold Nugget; Proker (F_1); Smallpak (Sutton's); Tender and True (Sutton's); White Custard; Yellow Custard; Zucchini (F_1).

Trailers Little Gem; Long Green;

Below left: One of the most reliable magnolias for the small garden is M. soulangeana

Below: 'Tender and True', a bush variety of marrow

*'Long Green', one of several
trailing marrow varieties*

Long White; Table Dainty (Sutton's);
Vegetable Spaghetti.

Sowing Although seeds may be sown
outdoors in mid-May where the plants
are to grow it is more customary to
give them an earlier start by sowing
under glass. Plants must not be set outdoors (unless cloche protection is given)
until all danger of a night spring frost
has passed. Early June is usually the
right time to set marrow plants out in
the garden. A bush plant needs $2\frac{1}{2}$ sq.
ft. of room; a trailer needs much more
if permitted to roam over the ground.
Plants of trailing varieties may be
planted at 15 in. apart alongside a 6-ft.
high trellis. This may be a wire mesh
fence, plastic or wire garden netting or
nylon bean netting. Trailers also grow
well on 'wigwams' made by pushing
four strong poles or bamboo canes in
the soil, tying them near the apex and
winding soft wire or string around the
structure. Marrow plants need no pruning apart from the removal of the central growing point of the main leader of
trailers when the leaders reach the top
of the supports. Keep down weeds,
water often in dry weather and if the
soil is not very rich apply liquid
manure feeds when marrows are swelling. Fertilization of female marrow
flowers is usually carried out by pollinating insects. Some gardeners like to
make sure of fertilization by doing the
job themselves. To hand pollinate wait
until midday. Then pick a male flower,
strip off the petals and twist the single
'core' of the male flower into the
divided 'core' of a female flower.
These have small marrows at their rear.

Mesembryanthemum
The Livingstone Daisy (Half-hardy
Annual) 6 in.
Of South American origin, this annual,
almost always sold under the name
mesembryanthemum, but correctly
known as *Dorotheanthus bellidiflorus*,
requires the maximum sun and a rather
dry soil. Of spreading habit, it is most
decorative trailing over a dry wall or
growing in crazy paving. Sow under
glass in March or April and plant out in
May. There is a wide range of colours.

Michaelmas Daisy
Aster
The garden would be dull in autumn
if no Michaelmas daisies were to be
seen. One can only emphasize the need
to choose varieties which do not need
staking, and to replant every three
years, using only the outer healthier
shoots. Spring is the best time to divide
asters.

Those species suitable for rock gardens do well in open, sunny positions
and in any good, well-drained soil.
They may be increased by seeds or by
division of old plants. Most flower in
mid to late summer. *A. alpinus* has large
blue and gold aster flowers on 9-in.
stems. There is a nice white form and
'Beechwood' has large more richly
coloured flowers but is less 'alpine' in
appearance. *A. natalensis* has flowers
of gentian blue on 6-in. stems.

The Livingstone daisy,
Mesembryanthemum
criniflorum (*botanically known
as* Dorotheanthus bellidiflorus)

Nasturtium

Tropaeolum (Hardy Annual) 9-in. Trailing and Climbing

T. majus varieties are easily grown provided simple rules are observed. Do not sow too early as the seedlings may be ruined by a late frost; poor soil is preferable to rich which will encourage leaf growth to hide the flowers. Late April is time enough to sow where they are to flower in southern England. There are single, semi-double and double flowered varieties in shades of glowing scarlet, golden-yellow, cherry-rose, mahogany-red and mixed colours.

Nicotiana

Tobacco Plant (Half-hardy Annual) 1½-in.

Fragrance is one of the chief attractions as the flowers usually open in the evening, although if grown in partial shade they often remain open all day. 'Sensation' is a strain with flowers of mixed colours that do remain open in daylight. 'Lime Green' has unusual greenish-yellow flowers, popular for floral arrangements. Sow under glass in a moderate temperature in March. Plant out, when the risk of frost is past, in rich moist soil.

Onions

Onions do best in a medium loam or reasonably light soil, provided that it does not dry out excessively.

Onions from Sets An easy way of growing maincrop onions is by planting 'sets' (small immature onions) during the second half of March. After digging rake the site level and simply press sets in the loose soil 9 in. apart, in rows 1 ft. apart.

Onions from Seed In late August sow seeds thickly in a 1-in. drill. It pays to protect with cloches from October to early March. Dig up all the young plants in March and transplant them 9 in. apart in good rich soil. Do not plant deeply. 'Giant Zittau' and 'A.1' are good varieties for August sowings. Alternatively, in late March/early April sow seeds fairly thickly in 1-in. deep drills, 1 ft. apart.

Varieties 'Ailsa Craig'; 'A.1'; 'Autumn Queen'; 'Bedfordshire Champion'; 'Big Ben'; 'Cranston's Excelsior'; 'Crossling's Selected'; 'Endura'; 'Giant Zittau'; 'James's Long Keeping'; 'Superba'; 'Unwin's Reliance'; 'Up-to-Date'; 'Wijbo'.

The flowering tobacco plant

Hoe and hand weed. Start thinning spring-sown seedlings in June and continue doing so until mid-July. Plants left to bulb up should be around 9 in. apart.

The maggots of the onion fly burrow into young onions. The foliage withers and the plants die. Autumn-sown onions and those grown from sets are unlikely to be affected, spring-sown seedlings are likely to be damaged in June and July. Female onion flies find onion plants by their odour. Prevent broken roots and foliage during thinning by watering beforehand if the soil is dry. Bury unwanted thinnings in the compost heap or the ground. Avoid breaking onion foliage when hoeing. Hoe occasionally to keep down weeds. Water generously in dry weather. Liquid feeds may be given weekly when bulbs are swelling, but overfeeding will lead to onions which will not store well.

When in August the foliage yellows and topples over on to the soil, stop watering and feeding. When the foliage is brown, dry and brittle, just lift the onions off the ground. Hang the onions in bunches in full sun for a week; when they are quite dry, rub off dead roots, dry soil and very loose scales. Store in a cold place such as an unheated greenhouse, a garden shed or a garage, in trays, or, better still, roped.

Salad Onions

Although thinning of spring-sown onions are of use in early summer salads, 'White Lisbon' is grown solely for salad use. Sow seeds in August or March, quite thickly. Use thinnings as soon as they are large enough.

Pickling Onions (Shallots)

These are generally grown for pickling, although they may be used in soups and stews. As soon as the soil dries somewhat in March, push bulbs into it, 9 in. apart, in rows 1 ft. apart. Keep the rows weed free. Lift the clumps in July, separate the bulbs and spread them out to dry. Store in a cool place. There are also brown-skinned ('Brown Pickler') and white-skinned ('Paris Silver Skin') onions for pickling. Sow seeds quite thickly in March in a ½-in. deep drill. Keep down weeds and dig the crop when the foliage withers.

Garlic

Plant 'cloves' (segments of garlic bulbs) 6 in. apart, 1 in. deep in a sunny site during February or March. Dig the crop when the foliage dies.

Peony
Paeonia (Hardy Perennial)

Among the longest lived of all perennials, peonies should be planted with permanence in mind. They need space in which to expand in an open situation. They like a rich deep soil and respond to mulching. Old plants can be divided, between August and October, carefully using a knife to separate the most vigorous chunks. Planting depth is important; the new buds should rest 1 in. below the surface. Varieties of the

*The spring-flowering peony
'Lady Alexandra Duff'*

popular June-flowering Chinese peony *(P. lactiflora)*, up to 3 ft. tall, have huge flowers in shades of pink, red and white, single, semi-double and double. Some are more fragrant than others. Consult a reliable catalogue for details of the numerous varieties. *P. officinalis* is the old cottage garden peony, 2 ft. tall, with very fragrant flowers, usually double, in red, crimson, pink and white.

Pansy
Viola (Hardy Biennial) 6–9 in.

Violas usually have smaller flowers than pansies, often self-coloured, are of tufted habit and are best treated as hardy biennials. Sow both kinds in seed boxes in a cold frame in June or July and keep the seedlings cool and moist. When large enough to handle prick the seedlings out in rows and in September or October plant out in flower beds. Do not let them dry out at any time. They like a rich moist soil, in sun or partial shade. Sowing can also be done in March or April in the open where they are to flower later the same year. There are numerous special strains, also winter-flowering varieties.

Viola *V. cornuta*, the horned violet, bears graceful long-spurred lavender-mauve flowers on 6-in. stems. Grow from cuttings or seed. It grows in any good soil and sunny place; *V. cucullata*, 4 in., loves shade and carries large white, lilac-veined 'violet' flowers in spring. Increase by division every two or three years.

Papaver
Poppy

For size of flower, *P. orientalis*, the Oriental poppy, can easily compete with peonies. For brilliance of colour, they can excel them, but they are not so permanent. All flower from late May until late June. The most erect is the blood-red 'Goliath', 3–3½ ft., though the orange-scarlet 'Marcus Perry' is nearly as erect. Other varieties are brownish-red, various shades of pink, also white. All like a very well-drained soil, not too rich. Their fleshy roots are brittle and any pieces left when old plants are dug out will sprout again. Propagation is by 3-in. long root cuttings in spring.

The 'Jersey Gem' violet

The annuals are easily raised from seed; the diverse annual poppies should be sown in March, April and May where they are to flower. Shirley poppies, derived from *P. rhoeas*, may also be sown in September to flower from May onwards. From the opium poppy, *P. somniferum*, have been raised many fine varieties, including double peony-flowered and double carnations. The charming alpine poppy, *P. alpinum*, is a short-lived plant but it perpetuates itself by means of self-sown seedlings in sunny places and light, gritty soil. The leaves appear in tiny tufts, surmounted throughout the summer by miniature poppy flowers.

The 'Pink Chiffon' poppy

Parsnip

Most gardeners favour a long-rooted parsnip such as 'Hollow Crown Improved' and 'Tender and True' (Sutton's). Shorter-rooted sorts are better where the garden top-soil is shallow. The new 'Avon-resister' has short, thick roots.

Sowing Parsnip seed may be sown as soon as the soil is workable in March or in April. Sow fairly thinly in 1-in. deep seed drills spaced at 12 in. apart. Pelleted seed is on offer. Sow pellets at 1 in. apart. Hoe to keep down weeds. Thin parsnip seedlings twice, first in April, to leave seedlings at about 1 in. apart, and again in late June when each plant left to grow on should be about 8 in. from its neighbours in the row. Dig parsnips for use as and when wanted during winter and early spring. Any parsnips still in the ground in March may be dug up and heeled in a trench.

Parsnip canker is a common physiological disorder of parsnips, not a disease. Brown patches occur on the parsnip skin. A bad attack leads to rot. If this is your problem in parsnip growing change to 'Tender and True' or 'Avon-resister'. Both show resistance to canker.

Bricks laid in running bond pattern to form a paved area

Paths and Patios

Paths have a most important role to perform in the garden because they are a means of access to various parts of the garden and they should be used also to link interesting sections of the layout. For instance, a path could be laid in the lawn close by a flower border to link with one of the main paths.

Paths should be kept to the minimum however, especially in the smaller gardens. A firm clear pathway to the coal bunker or to the shed or greenhouse is essential in most gardens and there should be, if possible, a main path which extends the full length of the garden. This is important for wheeling things on, especially in a new garden where some construction work will be going on for several seasons. There is always the tidying up of the garden each autumn and the use of the wheelbarrow is facilitated if a good path is provided.

Paths need not be uninteresting — they should be as colourful as possible or laid with an interesting pattern. Try to sweep or curve paths in the garden to add a pleasing appearance but do not make them too complex in their routes. It is well to remember that straight paths have a tendency to narrow a garden.

In the very small garden there may not be sufficient room to have many meandering paths, so the design or layout should concentrate all the more on the use of texture, colour and slab size variation.

There are several interesting materials which can be used most successfully for path-making. Slabs of one size are very popular and a path can be made quite quickly with these. Paving of several different sizes can be used to form an attractive design. Textured or 'natural-faced' surfaces to paving adds a weathered touch and provides a path which has a good non-slip surface. Exposed aggregate surfaces are available in the more expensive paving and these are very attractive indeed. A curving or winding path is more easily constructed if specially shaped slabs are laid. These can be quickly laid to form a very appropriate path in the natural or cottage garden type of garden setting. Hexagonal paving produces a very interesting pattern and is very easy to lay. Special pieces are available so that a straight edge can be given to a path. This type of paving will produce a wider path than usual owing to the size of the slab and the need to use extra pieces to form the straight edge. Individually, these slabs form an interesting and unusual stepping-stone path when set in a lawn.

Old bricks can form a useful path although the work of construction will be somewhat slow because of the small size of the material used. Numerous different patterns can be created and the bricks blend in well with the informal type of garden layout.

Pebbles, unusual path-making materials, are ideal for forming different patterns and textures. They are best laid in small blocks here and there in a path and should be placed where they will not be walked on as their surface is uneven.

Paths can be made from cold tarmacadam which can be purchased in bags. Do not overlook the invaluable crazy paving or broken paving.

Round paving stones in various colours are available and these can be used to form a stepping-stone path in the lawn.

When a path is made from concrete only it is a good idea to provide it with a slight curve or camber so that water is shed to each side.

One feature which should be included in most garden layouts is a paved area. There are several good reasons why this feature is worth consideration. Firstly it will provide a place for relaxation and leisure where meals can be taken outdoors in the summer months. Secondly it will enhance the garden a great deal by its colour and texture. Finally, it will be a labour-saving part of the garden because a well-laid paved area is weed free.

There is, also of course, the considerable pleasure, interest and sense of achievement one gets from a do-it-yourself feature and this type of design can save quite a lot of money if it is constructed by the gardener himself.

Pears

These have requirements generally similar to those of apples but flourish best in a somewhat heavier and moister soil. They are slightly more tolerant of indifferent drainage. When on quince rootstock they are very susceptible to iron deficiency on chalky soil.

The Care of Pears

Pears blossom a little earlier than apples and therefore there is a slightly higher risk of damage by frost or inadequate pollination because the weather discourages the pollinating insects from flying. They often take somewhat longer than apples to settle down and start fruiting. Pears may be grown in any of the forms in which apples are grown.

Pruning Bush Trees

At first prune as for apples but more lightly, but when regular cropping starts, pruning needs to be harder than for apples, leaders being reduced by two-thirds to three-quarters, laterals to three buds and sub-laterals to one. Pears form natural spurs more readily than do apples but a few varieties – notably 'Jargonelle', 'Josephine de Malines' and 'Packham's Triumph' are tip-bearers and these must be pruned much more lightly with all short laterals left uncut to form a terminal fruit bud.

Pruning Cordons, Dwarf Pyramids, Espaliers and Fans

As for apples, except that the new shoots will mature earlier.

Right: For precast paving it is advisable to choose fairly quiet, muted colours and to use one colour only

Below: 'Louise Bonne of Jersey', a dessert pear

Fruit Thinning

Generally less thinning of pears is required than of apples. Size of fruit will be improved and regularity of cropping aided if glut crops are thinned to one or, occasionally, two fruitlets per spur.

Watering

In dry weather watering will be necessary, particularly when the trees are young. A spring mulch will help.

Picking

The test for readiness to pick is the same as for apples, but pears need to be handled with even more caution as they bruise remarkably easily and the spurs are very brittle. The earliest varieties will be ready in late July or early August and should be eaten at once. Do not wait for pears to become soft before picking. 'Williams' Bon Chretien', for example, should be picked when still hard but will soon ripen.

Storing

Polythene bag storage is not so successful with pears but they will keep indoors in a slightly drier atmosphere and higher temperature than apples. Be careful not to pick the late-keeping varieties too soon. They are better laid out separately on shelves rather than wrapped and stored in boxes. When almost ripe they should be brought into a living room to finish.

Feeding

Pears often need more nitrogen than do apples and are less liable to suffer from potash shortage. Normally the ground around them should be clean cultivated and mulched in spring with rotted farmyard manure or garden compost. Where no natural manure or compost is available, mulch with peat after first dressing with 1 oz. of sulphate of ammonia, 2 oz. of superphosphate and $\frac{1}{2}$ oz. of sulphate of potash per sq. yd.

Rootstocks for Pears

Years ago pears were grown on their own roots or on a seedling pear rootstock. These made very large trees and sometimes took 20 years or more to start fruiting – hence the phrase 'plant pears for your heirs'. Pear stocks are only used nowadays for standards and half-standards. For garden culture pears are now budded on quince rootstocks which restrict growth and induce early fruiting. Unfortunately some varieties of pear are not compatible with quince and in such cases the stock is 'double-worked', budded or grafted first with a variety which is compatible and then with the desired variety.

Malling Quince C Most dwarfing (although not so markedly dwarfing as M.1X used for apple). May be used for bush trees, cordons or dwarf pyramids.
Malling Quince A More vigorous than Quince C and should be used for bush trees, cordons or dwarf pyramids where the soil is poor, and, on good soil, where a larger tree is required.

Pears for Every Season
(From August to April)
August Jargonelle (2) D, T.
September Gorham (3) D; Williams' Bon Chretien (2) D, F.
September–October Bristol Cross (3) D, NP; Fertility Improved (.) D-P; Fondante d'Automne (2) D, F; Merton Pride (2) D, F, T.
October Baronne de Mello (2) D, F; Beurre Hardy (3) D; Beurre Superfin (2) D, F; Louise Bonne of Jersey (1) D.
October–November Conference (2) D; Emile d'heyst (1) D; Pitmaston Duchess (3) C, T; Seckle (1) D, F; Thompson's (2) D, F.
November–December Doyenné du Comice (3) D, F; Packham's Triumph (2) D, F.
November–January Winter Nelis (3) D, F.
December–January Glou Morceau (3) D, F; Josephine de Malines (2) D, F; Vicar of Winkfield (1) C, T.
December–April Catillac (3) C, T.
March–April Easter Beurre (1) D.
Notes (1) (2) (3) These figures indicate flowering time. C – Cooker; D – Dessert; D-P – Dual purpose; F – Recommended for fine flavour; T – Triploid. Such varieties will not pollinate others and it is necessary to plant two other non-triploid (diploid) varieties in the same flowering group, one to pollinate the triploid, the other to fertilize the pollinator. N P – Has no good pollen and cannot pollinate others. (.) This is a tetraploid, a special case and self-fertile.

Note that Fondante d'Automne, Louise Bonne of Jersey, Seckle and Williams' Bon Chretien will not pollinate each other.

Peas

Soil These vegetables need well-drained soil which is not at all acidic. Should a soil test show acidity, apply lime (ground chalk) at the rate of from $\frac{1}{2}$ to 1 lb. per sq. yd. after winter digging. Simply sprinkle the lime over the dug soil. No manure or garden compost need be applied to the sites where peas

Harvest peas when the pods are well filled and firm

and beans are to grow. Choose a site which was enriched with manure or garden compost for a different crop grown in the previous summer. Land in which potatoes or winter cabbage was grown is suitable.
Sorts of Peas There are two main groups of garden peas. Hardiest are round-seeded; slightly less hardy but with a reputation for their superior flavour are varieties with wrinkled seeds. These are known as 'marrowfats'. There are many different pea varieties. These are divided into three sections: First Early; Second Early; Maincrop.
When to Sow
First Early Late October: in colder parts cover the row with cloches and keep cloches in position until late April. Early February: in large pots in a warm

greenhouse. March: outdoors or under cloches. Remove cloches in late April. Early April: outdoors. Late June: outdoors and always keep well-watered in dry weather.

Second Early   April: outdoors.

Maincrop   Late April/May: outdoors.

Some Popular Garden Peas

(The height given is the average for the plant.)

First Early   Early Bird 1½ ft.; Feltham First 1½ ft.; Foremost 3 ft.; Forward 2 ft.; Gradus 3 ft.; Hurst Beagle 1½ ft.; Kelvedon Viscount 2 ft.; Kelvedon Wonder (q.f.) 1½ ft.; Little Marvel (q.f.) 1¼ ft.; Meteor 1½ ft.; Pilot 3 ft.; Progress 1½ ft.; Sleaford Phoenix 1½ ft.; Sweetness 3 ft.; Topcrop (q.f.) 2½ ft.

Second Early   Achievement 5 ft.; Early Onward (q.f.) 2 ft.; Giant Stride 2 ft.; Kelvedon Climax 2½ ft.; Kelvedon Monarch (q.f.) 2½ ft.; Kelvedon Spitfire 2 ft.; Shasta (q.f.) 2½ ft.; Show Perfection (q.f.) 5 ft.

Maincrop   Alderman 5 ft.; Histon Kingsize 3½ ft.; Histon Maincrop 2½ ft.; Lincoln 2 ft.; Lord Chancellor 3 ft.; Onward (q.f.) 2 ft.; Recette (q.f.) 2 ft.

Note   q.f. – Suitable for quick-freezing, should you have a surplus.

How to Sow   Garden peas are sown where the plants are to grow. Before sowing rake the soil surface level, removing all large stones and clods. A popular way of sowing peas is to take out an 8-in. wide furrow, using a draw hoe. Use a garden line to have a straight row and make the furrow no more than 1 in. deep in heavier soils; 2 in. deep, but no more, in light soils. Should the soil not be wet, flood the furrow with water.

Start sowing after the water has drained away. Pea seeds are quite large. Sprinkle them fairly evenly on to the flat bottom of the furrow so that each seed is about 2½ in. from the next. After sowing use a rake to draw soil over the seeds and to fill the furrow at the same time gently firming the soil.

Some birds will take pea seeds and will hunt for them after they have been sown; other birds peck at pea seedlings. Cloches give automatic protection against bird attacks. For open garden sowings, several strands of black cotton stretched around and over the rows immediately after sowing provide full protection.

Secure the cotton to short bamboo canes on either side of the rows. A rough, ready and fairly accurate guide to the distance between rows is to space them to the height of the variety.

Do not waste large spaces between pea rows; grow lettuces or various members of the cabbage tribe in them.

Cultivation   Where black cotton is used to prevent bird damage the cotton also serves as an excellent support for short growing (dwarf) peas. For varieties growing taller than 3 ft. augment the black cotton with brushwood or with strings tied to tall canes. Hoe between rows to prevent weeds. Pull out weeds growing in the rows by hand when the pea plants are young.

In dry weather water often and water well. Pea plants which are short of water are prone to several disorders. The worst pest of garden peas is the pea moth. This is attracted to pea plants weakened by lack of moisture at the roots. Mulching pea rows with straw can reduce the amount of watering necessary in hot, dry summer weather.

Pelargoniums and Geraniums

Pelargoniums

The pelargonium is one of the most popular of flowers. It is native to South Africa, Australia and Turkey, but is now widely grown in the temperate areas of the world.

Of the several sub-divisions of the genus the following six are the most popular.

(1) *Zonals (P. hortorum)*   Commonly but incorrectly known as 'geraniums', these are widely grown in beds, greenhouses, tubs, urns, borders, etc. Foliage may be zoned or plain, flowers single, double or semi-double, colours ranging from white through all shades of salmon and pink to reds and purples.

Included in this section are Irenes, Deacons, Rosebuds, Cactus and Stellar varieties, detailed as follows:

The scarlet-flowered zonal pelargonium 'Gustav Emich'

IRENES   This vigorous strain produces larger flower heads in greater abundance than older varieties. Flowers are produced on long stems making them particularly suitable for arrangements and cut flowers, and are all semi-double. Spaced at not less than 18-in. intervals for correct development in beds and borders, the best results are obtained by planting first into 5-in. clay pots and sinking the pots into the ground.

DEACONS (often known as Floribunda Geraniums)   Derived from a cross between an ivy-leaf and a miniature, these are more compact than Irenes and produce many more smaller flower heads. The development of the plant may be controlled by the pot size: for instance a plant in a 5-in. pot will grow to about 1 ft. in diameter, whereas one in a 15-in.

pot may develop to about 4 ft. in diameter.

ROSEBUD AND CACTUS VARIETIES The former bear relatively small flowers and the petals never fully open, thus looking like rosebuds. There are five varieties, three shades of red, one medium purple and one white with pink edges to the petals and a green centre. Cactus varieties have narrow twisted petals rather like quills. Colours range through white, salmon and pink to red, orange and purple.

STELLAR VARIETIES Available in both single and double varieties, they originated in Australia. The foliage is star-shaped (hence the name), sometimes zoned but often unmarked, and the flowers are carried on long stems. Plants seldom reach more than 18 in. in height in Britain but will grow to over 5 ft. in Australia and California.

(2) *Fancyleaf Zonals* These are mainly grown for their unusual leaf colouring, the flowers often (but not always) being insignificant, usually red, single and sparsely produced.

Popular for bedding schemes, they are also widely used for edging borders and to add variety to mixed groups. Leaf colouring ranges from green-and-black, various shades of green, yellow and bronze to red and copper in a variety of combinations. Because they are seldom as bushy as the Irenes or Deacons, a more impressive effect is produced by spacing them 8–9 in. apart.

(3) *Regals (P. domesticum)* These are commonly known in Britain and Australia as pelargoniums and in the U.S.A. as show or Lady Washington geraniums. They are mainly grown in this country as pot plants and greenhouse plants but they are suitable for outside beds, borders and tubs in sheltered but sunny positions. Flowering depends upon light to a large extent; if the quality of winter light is sufficient they can be flowered throughout the year; if the light is poor they will rest.

Colours range from white to near-black through every possible shade and combination of shades except yellow and pure blue. The flowers are usually larger than those of the zonals and the leaves are unzoned. However, there are now at least two varieties with coloured foliage.

Left: The Regal pelargonium 'Mrs E Aickman'

'Mrs Quilter', a fancyleaf pelargonium

(4) *Ivyleaf Varieties (P. peltatum)* The fleshy leaves of these are shield-shaped. Flowers may be single, semi-double or double. These trailing varieties are mainly used in Britain for hanging baskets, tubs and urns, but are widely planted in other countries in bedding schemes for ground cover. Foliage may be zoned or plain, and there are a few fancy-leaved varieties, including 'Crocodile', with a mesh-like pattern over the foliage in white or cream. Colours range through white, salmon and pink to reds and purple.

(5) *Scented-leaf Varieties* There are hundreds of these since they seed readily and produce many forms with only slight variations. The aroma is released when the foliage is brushed or gently pinched with the fingers. In California and South Africa they can make bushes up to several feet in diameter, but in Britain they are normally grown as pot plants or in the greenhouse and seldom reach more than 2 ft. in height, although plants of 'Mabel Grey' have been grown to nearly 6 ft. Flowers are usually insignificant.

(6) *Miniatures and Dwarfs* These are mostly zonals, double, semi-double and single varieties in colours ranging from white through salmon and pink to reds and purples. This classification covers mature plants normally less than 8 in. high, chiefly grown as greenhouse pot plants but they can be used very effectively in bedding schemes, wall pockets and borders. Cultivation is as for other groups but over-potting should be avoided if maximum flower is desired. They can be flowered throughout the year under the correct conditions. The colour range is as for zonals. There are

a few miniature regals all with mauve or purple-and-white flowers, and two miniature ivy leaves – 'Gay Baby' with tiny white flowers, and 'Sugar Baby' with pink flowers.

General Culture All pelargoniums prefer a sunny position, medium loam and shelter from north and north-east winds. They will withstand a wide temperature range. Propagation is by cuttings, 3–4 in. long, taken from green shoots, preferably in late July or early August (cuttings from miniatures will be shorter). Over-watering should be avoided; plants can easily be killed by any excess of water. Regular feeding with a balanced fertilizer is beneficial but avoid high-nitrogen feeds including animal manures, which will result in lush growth and few flowers.

Pelleted Seeds

These make sowing easier because the pellets may be handled separately and placed at a distance from each other in the seed drill. This replaces the old method of mixing such small vegetable seeds as carrots and lettuce with sand.

Because pelleted seeds are evenly spaced, each seedling has room for good development.

Moisture must be present for the germination of all vegetable seeds. Where pelleted seeds are sown, even more moisture must be present to encourage the clay of the pellets to disintegrate quickly and permit rapid germination. Unless the soil is already very wet, always, soak seed drills with water before sowing pelleted seeds.

Petunia

(Half-hardy Annual) 9–15 in.
Modern hybrid petunias are available in many different types: large-flowered singles and doubles, compact bedding varieties, pendulous forms suitable for hanging baskets or window boxes, bicolours, self-colours, some with fringed and ruffled flowers. They are sun-loving plants, although some of the new varieties are colourful even in a poor summer. The vigorous F_1 hybrids, with large trumpet-shaped flowers of uniform colour are outstanding. Sow the seed under glass in March and grow the seedlings on steadily without a check. Prick out in boxes when large enough to handle and grow them on in the greenhouse. Put them in a cold frame to harden off before planting out in late May or early June.

Phlox

The annual *Phlox drummondi* is a popular, free-flowering bedding plant in shades of pink, salmon, crimson, violet and purple, many with a striking white eye; there are also pure white varieties. The compact varieties are about 6 in. high and the 'Grandiflora' hybrids up to 1 ft. Sow the seed in gentle heat in March and plant out from mid-May onwards in a sunny position, to flower from July until early October. Keep the young plants well watered.

Hardy Perennials Among the brightest of border plants, phlox are happiest in light rather than heavy soil.

They should be divided every three years, or propagated by root cuttings to avoid attacks by phlox celworm. The best dwarf white is still 'Mia Ruya'; 'White Admiral' at 3 ft. is taller. 'Mother of Pearl', 3 ft., is a vigorous, weather-proof pink suffused white; 'Mies Copijn' is soft pink and 'Dodo Hanbury Forbes' is somewhat deeper, with 'Windsor' a carmine-rose shade. 'Endurance', salmon-rose, 'Brigadier', orange-salmon; 'Spitfire' and the intensely bright 'Prince of Orange' should not be missed. The most reliable deep red is 'Starfire', with 'Tenor' an early flowering blood-red; 'Aida', 'San Antonio' and 'Vintage Wine' are in the magenta range, with 'The King', 'Parma Violet' and 'Marlborough' for violet-purples. Lavender-blue shades include 'Skylight' and 'Hampton Court'.

There are many important rock garden plants in this large genus. The species, selections and hybrids, loosely grouped as 'cushion phloxes', provide invaluable colour early in the year, are of neat habit, easily grown in any good, well-drained soil and benefit from being closely trimmed after they have flowered. Propagate by cuttings or

Above left: Phlox douglasii

Above: The numerous varieties of herbaceous phlox provide brilliant colour for many weeks in late summer

division of old plants in spring or autumn. The most popular are the forms of *P. subulata*. All are sun-lovers and, although they will grow in light shade, they do not as a rule flower freely unless given full light. *P. adsurgens* is an exception in that it prefers a slightly shaded position. Its 3–4 in. mats are decorated by large, salmon-pink flowers; *P. amoena* has 6-in. stems which carry heads of purple flowers. There is a form with pretty, variegated foliage; *P. divaricata* is of rather loose, untidy habit but the large lilac flowers are carried in loose heads on 12–15 in. stems; the forms of *P. douglasii* are of close, cushion-forming habit and carry carpets of almost stemless flowers. Among the best are 'Boothman's Variety', with clear mauve flowers, 'Rosea', rich pink and 'Snow Queen', pure white; *P. stolonifera* 'Blue Ridge', 12 in., is a lovely phlox with heads of clear blue flowers; *P. subulata* has several forms and it should be plentifully represented on every rock garden. They are also excellent plants for growing in walls, crazy paving, or for tumbling over a path-edge. They all make wide, low cushions covered with flowers; 'Appleblossom', soft pink; 'Fairy', small, neat flowers of lavender with deeper colour marking the base of the petals; 'G. F. Wilson', one of the oldest and still one of the best with mauve flowers; 'Model', rose-coloured flowers; 'Pink Chintz', clear soft pink blossoms; 'Temiscaming', brilliant magenta-red, are excellent varieties.

Planning Your Garden

When planning a garden consider very carefully the exact role the garden is to play in your life.

First there are the obvious needs: a place for children to play, room to sit in sun or shade, a washing line, a vegetable patch, space for cutting flowers, a working area for bonfires and compost heaps, a workshop or toolshed, are just a few elements.

Then there are the more elaborate requirements: a swimming pool, a tennis court, a croquet lawn, a sauna cabin, a greenhouse, a rose garden, a rock garden, orchard, lily pool. Each of these is a major element round which a whole scheme might be evolved.

Less obvious, but still vitally important, are other basic human needs which are often forgotten today with fatal results in terms of human happiness. The need for privacy, not just from neighbours but from other members of the family. However harmonious our family life, there is often the need to be alone and the garden is an ideal setting for solitary thought.

So what do you really want? Only you can make the decision. So much depends on the way you live, the amount of time and money you are prepared to spend on maintaining the garden afterwards, and the specific problems you are presented with.

Above: A well-placed seat in a quiet corner

Left: In this small town garden there are no well-defined boundaries

Illusion is important and the smaller the garden the greater the need to use all available arts to make it seem larger and more interesting than it really is. Bad proportions can be improved, ugly features hidden, small spaces enlarged and apparent privacy achieved by simple means.

It can be an interesting experience looking at your potential garden from outside and realizing how much you can improve the general view for others. A carefully placed tree might hide drainpipes or a view of washing, or break up the long perspective of a dull street to make it seem more interesting. An urn or a patch of bright colour seen through a gateway might make all the difference at the end of a cul-de-sac, while in the wider view careful planting to conceal the hard lines of boundaries might help to blend a new garden into the countryside. Often, visiting an unfamiliar area, it is the minor, unexpected touches which please most. A sudden cascade of roses over the top of a wall, the spray of a fountain in a patch of sunlight, an inviting garden path framed by trees. We forget that these effects were planned by someone and that we are often in a similar position to give pleasure to others.

Many new gardens are quite bare, but when an old garden has been split up into smaller plots, or some other site redeveloped, there are generally some existing trees and shrubs whose position, level in relation to surrounding ground and general size, shape and species (if known) should be carefully noted. Never destroy an existing plant, however poor or common it may seem, until you are quite sure that it cannot be incorporated in the new plan. Even if the final scheme does not require it, an existing shrub or tree, already established and probably capable of improvement by careful pruning and shaping, can give an immediate air of maturity while the new planting grows up. After five or ten years, if it is no longer needed, it can be removed.

Plums

The Care of Plums and Gages

Plums and gages may be grown as standards, half-standards, bushes, pyramids and fans. They are unsatisfactory as cordons or espaliers. They do best on deep heavy loam or on a well-drained clay soil. Ex-vegetable plot soil (rich in nitrogen) is excellent. Light soil results in poor fruit quality, brittle branches and a short life.

Plums are extremely susceptible to a fungoid disease known as silver leaf which is most infectious during the winter months. Pruning should be carried out during the summer, in spring or in early autumn immediately after the crop has been picked.

Pruning Bush Trees

First Year If a maiden is planted, behead it at about 3 ft. from soil level in spring just before growth starts. Existing feathers may be selected for the fruit branches if well spaced. Plums are very liable to branch breakage and it is important to select as branches laterals with a wide angle to the main trunk, these being much stronger than those which are more nearly vertical and make an acute angle with the stem.

Second Year In early spring cut back the selected branch leaders by a half.

Third Year Again cut leaders by a half of the previous season's growth.

Subsequent Years Between June and August remove crossing branches to open up the centre of the tree. Cut out any dead wood before mid-July. Some laterals may have to be cut out or shortened in summer to avoid overcrowding but otherwise plum pruning is best kept to a minimum. Should growth be poor, cut back some laterals drastically to encourage new wood. Plums fruit on second year wood and on spurs which will develop without your assistance on older wood.

Pruning Pyramids

The pyramid is the best form for plums in most gardens because it only needs 10 ft. of lateral space and can be restricted to a height of little more than 9 ft. You cannot buy plum trees already trained as pyramids so you must start with a maiden which should be on St. Julien A rootstock. Apart from size a great benefit with this type of tree is that branch breakage is substantially reduced and, with it, there is less possibility of silver leaf infection.

First Year In late March behead the maiden 5 ft. above the ground. Cut off at source any feathers up to a height of 18 in., and reduce those above that point to half their length. When the growth of new shoots ceases (about the third week in July) cut back branch leaders to 8 in., pruning just beyond a bud pointing downwards or outwards. Shorten laterals to 6 in.

Subsequent Years In April cut off two-thirds of the central leader's new growth. To keep the tree straight, cut to buds on opposite sides of the tree each year. When new growth ceases about the third week of July cut branch leaders to 8 in. and laterals to 6 in. Once the tree has reached 9 ft. cut the central leader to an inch or less of new growth each May. Should a new vertical shoot grow up to replace the central leader, remove it at source.

Pruning Fans
Form the framework of the fan in the manner described for peaches. When the tree reaches fruiting age, however, the treatment has to be slightly different as the plum fruits on old and new wood and one does not, therefore, have to cut back a lateral as soon as it has fruited. Any new laterals not required to extend the tree or to replace old laterals should be stopped when they have made six or seven leaves. It may be necessary to 'go over' the tree several times during the growing season for this pinching. Also rub out entirely any shoots pointing at the wall or directly away from it, doing this as soon as these unwanted growths are noticed.

As soon as the crop has been picked cut back by half all the laterals previously stopped and either tie down towards the horizontal any vigorous

'Victoria' plums

shoots growing vertically or cut them out entirely.

Fruit Thinning
With glut crops on bush or pyramid trees, the thinning of plums not only increases fruit size but reduces the risk of branch breakage and the entry of silver leaf disease. Proper thinning also promotes regular cropping.

Thin gradually in two stages, early in June and, later, after the natural crop during stone formation. Break or cut the fruitlets off so that stalks remain on the tree, eventually reducing dessert plums to a minimum spacing of 2 in. Cooking plums may be slightly closer.

Choice for the One-plum Garden
In many gardens there is room only for one plum tree and that must, therefore, be a self-fertile variety needing no other plum to pollinate it. Here are some of the best, all self-fertile, all dessert plums unless otherwise stated:

Above: 'Denniston's Superb' is a good plum for a small garden

Right: A fan-trained plum, 'Early Laxton'

Name	Ready to pick	Colour	Comment
Czar	Early August	Red-purple	Cooker. On small side but very heavy cropper. Reliable. Will grow on north wall.
Denniston's	Mid August	Greenish-yellow, red flush	Good regular cropper, fair gage flavour. Succeeds as a pyramid.
Early Transparent Gage	Mid August	Pale greenish-yellow with red dots	Very sweet and superb flavour but also makes first-class jam. Crops heavily and often needs thinning. One of the best.
Oullin's Golden Gage	Mid August	Straw-yellow with red dots	Large fruit, fair flavour. Also good for cooking, jam and bottling.
Victoria	Second half August	Carmine-rose with deeper red dots and pale blue bloom	Large fruits with good flavour when really ripe. Very heavy and regular cropper. Also first-class for all cooking or preserving.
Thames Cross	First half September	Golden yellow	Very large fruits. Fair flavour when ripe. Good for jam.
Merryweather	Second half September	Black	Cooker. Large fruit of damson flavour. Very good for bottling.
Severn Cross	Second half September	Golden yellow, pink flush, tiny red dots	Very large fruit. Sweet, fair flavour. Crops well.
Marjorie's Seedling	Late September/ October	Blue-black, deep blue bloom	Primarily cooker. Passable for dessert when ripe. Large fruits. Good and regular cropper.
Reine Claude de Bavay	Late September/ October	Pale lemon yellow, with white and sometimes red dots	Rich, gage flavour. Reliable cropper, sometimes heavy.

Potatoes

This is a useful crop to grow if you are starting from scratch. Potato plants are spreading in habit and smother weeds. A potato crop is often referred to as a 'cleaning crop' because the spreading habit and the cultivation carried out can eradicate many weeds.

The plant needs a well-drained soil, but one which retains moisture in dry summer weather. For potato growing the texture of both light and heavy soils is greatly improved by regular dressings of strawy manure or garden compost. The site chosen for potatoes should always be dressed with either of these plant food-rich soil improvers during winter digging, but never limed.

Planting

Seed potato tubers should be bought in winter and stood in trays to sprout. House the trays in a frostproof, light, cool, airy place. Good Friday is the traditional planting time but delay planting for up to a fortnight if the soil is too wet and cold.

Varieties

Potato varieties are divided into three groups: First Early; Second Early; Maincrop. All are planted at the same time.

First Early Arran Pilot*; Duke of York; Epicure; Home Guard*; Sharpe's Express; Ulster Chieftain*; Pollock's Pink Early*.

Second Early Craig's Royal*; Dr McIntosh*; Great Scot*; Maris Peer*; Maris Piper*; Pentland Dell*.

Maincrop Arran Banner*; Golden Wonder*; Kerr's Pink*; King Edward; Majestic*; Pentland Crown*.

*Immune against wart disease.

Only immune varieties should be planted in soils known to be infected with wart disease fungus. Never accept a gift of potatoes for planting in your garden if there is any chance that they were grown in soil infected with wart disease. Buy Ministry of Agriculture certified seed potatoes each season.

Use a garden line to make straight rows and use a draw hoe to make 6-in. deep furrows.

Planting distances	Distance between seed tubers in a row	Distance between rows
First Early	12 in.	2 ft.
Second Early and Maincrop	15 in.	2½ ft.

Discard any tubers which have not sprouted or which show decay. Plant so that the end of the tuber where most shoots are is uppermost. Rake soil over the tubers to fill the furrows.

Hoe between rows to keep down weeds. When the plants are 9 in. or so high, use a draw hoe to draw up soil around them. This practice is known as earthing-up. Some gardeners earth up again a few weeks later. After earthing up your potatoes do not use a hoe to remove weeds. Remove the few weeds which may appear by hand. In the drier, eastern half of the country the potato bed should be drenched with water off and on in dry summer weather.

Apart from wart disease, potato blight is the most feared disease among potato growers. This fungus is unlikely to be troublesome in a dry summer and is a greater worry in western parts of the country than in the drier east. Where blight is a normal hazard of potato growing, fortnightly sprayings with Bordeaux mixture, maneb or zineb are often necessary between early July and mid-September. A power sprayer is needed to ensure that all of the foliage is well-coated with one of these fungicides. A first early potato, such as 'Arran Pilot' is seldom affected by blight. Among maincrop potatoes, the new 'Pentland Crown' appears to resist blight.

Before harvesting first early varieties wait until flowers die and fall. The popular 'Arran Pilot' seldom blooms but imperfect flower buds form and fall. The digging of first earlies usually starts in late June. Dig only sufficient roots for immediate use. Continue digging as and when potatoes are required in the kitchen.

By mid-August all first earlies may have been dug. Second earlies may then be dug as and when potatoes are wanted. Lift the rest of second earlies along with maincrop in September.

Do not dig maincrop potatoes until the plants are brown, dry and shrivelled. Choose a dry, sunny day for digging the entire crop. Leave the tubers on top of the ground for an hour or so to allow them to dry.

Examine each tuber and put aside for immediate use any which are damaged. Store undamaged tubers only in boxes or trays in a dry, cool but frostproof place. Drape black polythene sheeting over the storage containers to prevent the potatoes from greening. Green potatoes are not edible.

Primulas

In this large genus there are species which are invaluable for growing under glass from which frost can be excluded. All can be raised from seed sown in spring. For sowing and potting use a slightly acid compost. *P. obconica* continuously produces clusters of large lilac, pink, crimson or white flowers. When some persons touch the foliage they are affected by a rash. The problem is overcome by wearing gloves. Sow from February to April. *P. malacoides* has dainty flowers produced in tiers. The colour varies from lavender to deep rose or white, some strains being double. Sow in June. *P. sinensis* has large single purplish-rose or white flowers. When potting do not bury the centres of the plants or they will decay. Sow in spring. *P. X kewensis* has fragrant yellow flowers in winter or early spring. Sow in March or April.

Do not leave the plants in small pots too long or they will starve, resulting in irregular development. Keep the soil in the pots firm but not hard.

P. acaulis is the primrose, of which there are many double flowered and coloured forms. They all like a cool position and deep, rich soil; *P. auricula*, 4 in., the alpine auricula, loves a sunny crevice from which to display its charming yellow, fragrant flowers; *P. denticulata* is a plant for a moist place. It has great heads of purple, crimson or white flowers on 1-ft. stems. *P. frondosa* makes tufts of soft, meal-covered leaves and has rounded heads of pink flowers on 4-in. stems; *P. minima*, one of the smallest, has tufts of glossy leaves and large pink flowers on 1-in. stems. It needs gritty soil. *P. marginata*, 6 in., is a fine crevice plant with white powdered leaves and heads of lavender flowers; *P. rosea* loves a really wet position such as a bog garden or by the edge of a stream. In early March it produces vivid carmine-red flowers on 6–9-in. stems.

Above: Primula vernales 'Wanda'

Below: Primula acaulis

Radishes

Those grown for summer salads vary in shape from round, through 'tankard' to long. Varieties are: 'Scarlet Globe', round; 'French Breakfast', tankard; 'Icicle', long; 'Yellow Gold', oval. Autumn/winter radishes are large; 'China Rose' and 'Black Spanish' are grated for salad use.

Sowing Sow in late March; for sowing under cloches choose 'Red Forcing' (Sutton's). For open ground sowings between late March and late July all summer varieties are suitable. Sow winter radish in mid to late July. Sow in fairly fertile soil, keep the plants moist and thin seedlings to 1 in. apart each

Above: A good selection of round radishes

way. Sow the large seeds of winter radishes 1 in. apart in 1-in. deep seed drills. Thin seedlings to 8 in. apart. Pull summer radishes as soon as some are sufficiently large for use. Pull winter radishes for use in autumn. Harvest those remaining in late October. Cut back the foliage to an inch from the radish and store the roots in sand in a shed or garage.

Right: Polyanthus pacific, *a robust strain*

Raspberries
The Care of Raspberries
Summer-fruiting raspberries bear their berries on new canes made the previous summer. On planting cut back the canes to 2 ft. and later in spring, when growth shows, cut back further to a live bud about 10 in. above soil level. This means you will get no crop the first summer but give the plants a chance to develop a good root system. No pruning will be necessary in the autumn following planting and the canes produced during that summer will give you your first crop in the second summer after planting. Thereafter, prune as soon as the crop has been picked, cutting all fruited canes to ground level, tying in up to six of the strongest new canes and removing any others. In February, tip the canes, reducing them to about 4 ft. 6 in. Stake and tie securely.

Autumn-fruiting varieties crop on the new canes which grew during the summer. Thus new plants cut down in April will try to fruit on the new canes the first year. Subsequently delay pruning until February and then cut all fruited canes to ground level.

The summer-fruiting varieties must be protected from birds and netting over the whole row is most satisfactory. By the autumn the birds have sometimes lost interest in this type of food and, in some areas at least, netting is unnecessary. Apart from this, and the time of pruning, summer and autumn raspberries need similar treatment.

Feeding Raspberries need a steady supply of nitrogen and potash. In the

Raspberries. Above: Lloyd George. Above left: Malling Exploit

first year a mulch of farmyard or stable manure (5 lb. per sq. yd.) put down in April will be sufficient but in subsequent years also give a dressing of 1 oz. per sq. yd. each of sulphate of ammonia and sulphate of potash in February. Every third year add 2 oz. per sq. yd. of superphosphate. Plenty of moisture is essential throughout the growing period and the hose may well have to be used in June. Keep weeds down but try not to disturb the surface soil more than is essential because this damages surface roots, for which reason a paraquat/diquat weedkiller is excellent. Such a weedkiller may also be used to destroy unwanted suckers which spring up away from the row.

A well-drained deep loam is the ideal but raspberries will also flourish in a light soil if top and second spit have been liberally enriched with moisture-holding vegetable matter and the soil is never allowed to dry out in drought. Good drainage is essential. Iron and manganese deficiencies can be serious on chalky soil.

Redcurrants
The Care of Red and White Currants
These are tolerant of most soils. They do best on a light loam but may show potash deficiency signs on a light sandy soil. They are less in need of rich humus content than other soft fruits and prefer only slight acidity. They are liable to iron deficiency on very chalky soil. They are both grown in the same way and there are also, but seldom seen, pink varieties. Their fruiting habit is quite different from the blackcurrant's and they, therefore, need quite different pruning. Redcurrants produce most of their fruit on short spurs on old wood and at the base of new growths. Little is borne on the new wood. As with gooseberries, birds can be a nuisance in winter, pecking out the buds. Otherwise delay pruning until early spring when, after first signs of growth are visible, you can make sure of pruning to sound buds.

Summer pruning a redcurrant bush

Pruning Bushes If a one-year-old bush is planted there may be three or four branches. Cut all back by two-thirds, to outward-pointing buds, so as to secure an open-centred bush.

In the second winter again cut back hard, by two-thirds, and remove entirely any ill-placed laterals. Shorten other laterals, not required as branches, to one bud.

By the third winter the bush should have sufficient main branches. In this and subsequent years shorten branch leaders by a half, always to outward-pointing buds. Shorten laterals to one bud.

'Blue Diamond', a dwarf rhododendron, suitable for the larger rock garden or the front of a border

Rhododendrons and Azaleas
(Medium growing, will not grow on chalk.)

In many modern catalogues, under this name (according to botanical rules) are included what we usually call azaleas (which are often, but not always, deciduous). Those we have long known as rhododendrons are evergreens.

None will tolerate lime and all prefer sandy and peaty soils. Many appreciate some shade and in general all dislike drought, particularly the evergreen kinds. All prefer protection from strong winds.

The roots are fine and fibrous, and naturally form balls, making them easy to plant and transplant. Plenty of peat should be worked in round this ball when planting, and the young plants should be well soaked. If, when planted, the bush shows a tendency to rock, it should be tied to a stake for a year or so.

One of the best azaleas is *R. luteum (Azalea pontica)*, a medium sized shrub covered with very sweetly scented yellow flowers in mid-May, the leaves turning a rich red in autumn. Smaller growing, with a much wider variation in colour, are the Mollis hybrids, and the Exbury and Ghent hybrids, usually flowering in May and also giving good autumn leaf colour. There are also the much smaller evergreen Japanese azaleas, mostly in pinks and reds and some white, opening from April to June. All these of the azalea group are suitable for moderate and small gardens.

The true rhododendrons are even more numerous and vary in size from trees to little shrubs. The common *R.*

ponticum (not to be confused with the so-called *Azalea pontica* mentioned above) is a large shrub with mauve to pink flowers. It is very common and is naturalized in places. There are many better kinds for gardens. A few well-known and reliable kinds are 'Pink Pearl', large rose-pink flowers, April–May; 'Fastuosum flore-pleno', semi-double flowers of an unusual bluish-mauve colour, May–June; 'Cynthia', deep rose with dark crimson markings, April–May; 'Britannia', fiery red flowers, April–May, and 'Mrs Furnival', soft-pink flowers with crimson blotches, May–June. These are all reliable and suitable for most gardens. There are many other dwarf kinds suitable for the edge of borders or rock gardens, including 'Blue Tit' (April–May) with blue flowers; *R. racemosum*, thickly covered with small rose-pink flowers at the same season; 'Blue Diamond' of erect growth with blue flowers in May and *R. campylocarpum*, also May-flowering with yellow blooms.

R. praecox is an erect shrub up to 3 ft. tall, with pink flowers opening in February if the weather is mild, but which may be frosted unless protected.

Rhubarb

The best variety is 'Timperley Early'. Plant stools in late autumn, 4 ft. apart. Do not pull sticks until the second season and always stop pulling at the end of June. Mulch the bed with compost or well-rotted manure each autumn.

Rock Gardens

The ideal site for a rock garden would be a gentle slope, on well-drained soil, falling to the south or west. Not many gardens will be able to provide such a perfect position, but there is no need to despair; many alternative situations will be quite satisfactory. Avoid if at all possible a due east aspect.

Site the rock garden right out in the open and never, if it can possibly be avoided, beneath overhanging trees, or in narrow alley-ways between adjacent buildings. Placed beneath trees, the plants will suffer from the shade cast by the branches above and the latter will be draughty. All plants hate draughts. Positions for plants which relish some shade can always be contrived, in the construction of the rock garden. An outcrop of rocks running east and west will provide a warm south face and a cool north aspect on the other side.

A detailed, stone-by-stone description of the making of a rock garden is almost impossible to write and quite impossible to follow in practice. So much depends upon each individual rock, the site, and what sort of scene is desired. One can really only set down some basic rules, which amount to a series of 'dos and 'don'ts'.

Do not set the stones in isolation over a mound of soil. This only creates a Victorian 'rockery' and there will be constant erosion of soil from higher to lower levels. Do not set stones up on edge so that they erupt from the soil like fangs. Instead lay them on their longest edge and make sure that they join in pleasant complexes or outcrops much as they would in nature on a hillside.

An alternative possible situation for alpine plants is between the cracks of paving stones. In fact, such a position provides everything that they like, such as a cool root run which does not dry out, their heads in the light and their collars protected from too much wet by the closely adjacent paving stones.

Retaining or free-standing walls also provide excellent homes for alpines. Here, too, they find perfect conditions. If all else fails, you have only to dig out a depth of soil in an open, sunny position, ensure good drainage and fill in with suitable compost and you have a bed which will grow a wide variety of them to perfection.

Those who are new to alpine gardening should start by growing the easier plants; those which will provide colour and interest over as long a period as possible. A criticism which has been aimed at rock gardens is that they are supremely beautiful and colourful in the spring and early summer, but deadly dull thereafter.

This need not be true; by choosing carefully from the immense variety of plants available rock gardens can be colourful from earliest spring until winter. There is, and always has been, a tendency to plant too many aubrietas, alyssums and arabis. These all blossom in the spring and are invaluable for providing masses of colour, but if they are too generously used, there are wide blank spaces for the rest of the year.

Any such vigorous and space devouring plants must be employed in moderation and ample space left for later flowering specimens. The beginner would do well to seek among such genera as *Dianthus, Campanula, Phlox, Gentiana, Primula, Helianthemum, Achillea, Saxifraga, Geranium, Iris, Lewisia, Ranunculus, Polygonum, Sedum* and *Sempervivum* in order to secure a succession of flowers throughout the summer and autumn.

A few really dwarf evergreen shrubs should also be grown. For this purpose none is better than the genuinely pygmy conifers. There is a trap here for the unwary however. Too often conifers are sold as dwarfs which will ultimately grow much too large for any rock garden.

Plants such as the cushion phloxes, helianthemums, aubrietas, arabis, alyssums, dianthus, veronicas, hypericums,

Right: Many colourful alpines may be grown in the crevices of a dry stone wall to create a wild effect

Below: A tight planting of begonias semperflorens, Southbank hybrids, along with cineraria maritima 'White Diamond'

iberis and geraniums benefit from being cut back quite severely after they finish flowering. This encourages new growth and often results in a further flush of late season blossom. It also maintains a tidy habit and prolongs the life of the plants.

Root Vegetables

Root vegetables do well in fertile garden soil but there should be no hard band of gravel or clay beneath the top spit nor should the top soil contain a high percentage of large stones. Often some deep digging is necessary to prepare a garden soil initially for first-class root vegetables. No manure or garden compost should be applied to spots in the garden where root crops are to be grown that season. Grow root crops in soil to which manure or garden compost was applied for a different crop in the previous season. Where potatoes or winter cabbage were grown are suitable sites for root crops. After the digging of the whole kitchen garden in winter or early spring just rake level and remove any large stones before sowing root vegetables. See 'The Kitchen Garden'.

Roses

Rose Beds

Conditions that Roses Like Fortunately roses are quite easy to accommodate. They have, however, several dislikes. These are poorly drained soil, deep shade, particularly when the roots of trees deprive them of nutriment, and very alkaline (chalky) soil.

Choosing a Site The site should be ideally in an open position, sunny for most of the day, preferably with some shade during part of the time. There should be no overhanging trees, although smaller shrubs often give the correct amount of shade and help to keep their roots cool.

Good Drainage The soil must be well drained, firstly, because roses dislike having their roots continuously in water and, secondly, well-drained soil stimulates the activity of the beneficial soil bacteria.

The drainage can be tested by digging a hole, 1 ft. deep and 1 ft. in diameter and filling it with water. If it does not empty away within a day, it is necessary to improve the drainage. This can often be done effectively by raising the bed with soil well above the level of the surrounding ground or by

digging a 2½-ft. deep trench across the bed and filling it with stones up to 1 ft. from the top and then with top-soil.

Roots of Roses Like other shrubs, the root system of a rose consists of two types of roots, viz., the tap-roots, which are long and strong so that they penetrate well into the soil, giving good anchorage and a lifeline to more distant sources of water and nutriment, when they are needed; and the surface roots, which emanate almost horizontally near the soil surface, collecting from the soil the rose's main supplies of moisture and plant foods.

The Ideal Soil for Roses Firstly, the top-soil must be friable so that the surface roots can pass freely through it. It must have a high fertilizer content, and not be easily washed away by rain, and it must be able to retain adequate water to assist the absorption of the necessary plant foods. Secondly, there should be beneath it a porous sub-soil, which is sufficiently broken up to allow the tap-roots to penetrate without hindrance. *Time of Planting* Bare-root roses can be planted at any time during the winter in open weather. Preferably it should be done, however, during October and November or from February onwards so as not to risk the possible deleterious effect of severe winter weather. Container-grown and pre-packed roses can be planted at any time, but during a dry period they should be copiously watered.

The distance apart roses are planted depends upon their vigour. Generally speaking, most bushes are satisfactory

Hybrid tea rose 'Grandpa Dickson'

when placed 20 in. apart, but for more vigorous ones, including species and shrub roses, this distance might be safely increased to 30 in. upwards, according to their ultimate span.

Roses need to be kept regularly fed, but like human beings and animals they do not want to be overfed, and certainly not with the wrong foods. What they like most of all is a well-planned diet given to them at the appropriate times of the year.

In addition roses are thirsty plants and need copious quantities of water. It is important to water whenever there is a dry spell, no matter how early in the season it might be, and not just during a heat wave, when their leaves are drooping, because by then it might be too late. A programme for feeding roses begins late in the winter after supplies of nutriments have become diminished. The first thing to do, preferably in February, provided the snows have gone, is to lay down a foundation for the future by distributing an organic fertilizer, which will break down over the ensuing months into simple chemical compounds and ensure that there is a basic supply that can be steadily absorbed by the plant. If it can be obtained, the substance to distribute is meat and bonemeal at the rate of two handfuls per square yard. Good substitutes are equivalent quantities of sterilized bonemeal, fish meal and John Innes Base Fertilizer.

Fertilizer is next applied in the spring, not earlier than April. This time it is a chemical fertilizer, which supplements the elements provided by the organic fertilizer, particularly when heavy rain has washed abnormally large quantities of a particular element away, or rapid growth, due to favourable weather conditions, has suddenly increase demand and so on. Generally, it is more satisfactory to put down a proprietary, ready-mixed rose fertilizer, of which there are several on the market. It is important to use one that is blended for roses and not a general fertilizer intended for vegetables. Such rose fertilizer is distributed in accordance with the manufacturer's instructions. Usually these mixtures contain the trace elements that are needed by roses.

Although it is a lot more trouble, gardeners may mix their own fertilizer for roses. A recommended mixture is: nitrate of potash 3 parts, sulphate of

ammonia 1½ parts, superphosphate of lime 8 parts, sulphate of potash 4 parts, sulphate of magnesium 1 part, sulphate of iron ¼ part. This is distributed at the rate of 2 oz. (about a handful) per sq. yd., once in April and again in May. Twenty pounds of this mixture is sufficient for 200 roses during the season.

It is important that no chemical fertilizer is applied after the end of July, otherwise lush growth might be produced, which will not withstand the winter.

Foliar Feeding This takes advantage of the fact that leaves absorb nutrients from liquids sprayed on them. It is not a substitute for the regular feeding programme, but something that can meet an emergency. There are several good foliar feeds on the market. They are best applied in the early morning or in the evening, but never in hot sun.

When to Prune With the exception of true ramblers, roses are pruned during the winter or early spring. Exactly when depends upon the location and degree of exposure of the garden. The proper time to prune such roses is when the sap is just beginning to rise. In the south and milder places this is usually February, while in northern and exposed gardens it can be up to six weeks later. At this time, the cut will heal quickly, but in late spring or early autumn, the shoot will bleed and, if a frost comes, damage is likely to be caused.

Ramblers are pruned in the late summer, soon after their flowers fade. So that they do not become unruly, the new shoots that remain should be tied in at the same time.

How to Prune If a rose of any sort is examined, it will be found that each of its shoots has growth buds, which alternately point in opposite directions, i.e. in a bush rose they are outwards and inwards towards its centre. In pruning a bush rose, the cut is made just above an outward-pointing bud, as it is desirable to keep the centre open with no inward-growing shoots crossing it, or where a horizontally-trained shoot of a climber is being pruned, it would be an upward pointing bud, because it is in this direction that growth is required.

The proper way to prune is to make a sloping cut, which begins level with

A beautiful display of red and pink climbing roses

the base of the bud on the side opposite to it and ends at a point on the same side as the bud, which is at a distance of $\frac{1}{4}$ in. from the base of the eye (see figure 9). The various types of roses should be pruned as described above but to different degrees and at different times.

Using Roses in the Garden
Hybrid Tea and Floribunda Roses These two types are those most commonly found in gardens. At one time, they were two very distinctly different sorts, with their own characteristics – the hybrid teas producing their flowers singly, or at most in threes, on each stem, and the floribundas, which were more usually single or semi-double, in clusters. However, rose breeders, by crossing hybrid teas and floribundas, and further intercrossing, have developed floribunda roses that have large clusters of perfectly formed hybrid tea shaped flowers. These are classified as 'Floribundas – hybrid tea type'. Also hybrid tea roses have been bred that produce their blooms in large clusters in much the same way as the floribundas. Excellent examples of these are 'Pink Favourite' and 'Fragrant Cloud'.

Polyantha-Pompons Where small areas are concerned, the almost forgotten, very hardy polyantha-pompoms, with their dainty clusters of colourful blooms, are valuable. They rarely grow more than 15 in. tall and can be usefully positioned in the foreground of mixed borders. Some varieties are subject to mildew, but 'Eblouissant', 'Ellen Poulsen', 'Jean Mermoz' and 'The Fairy' are far less susceptible.

Miniatures Even more diminutive are the miniature roses, ranging in height from the deep crimson 'Peon' at 5 in. to the clear yellow 'Bit o' Sunshine', which can reach 18 in. All have minute blossoms that are exact replicas of either hybrid tea or floribunda roses. They are excellent for forward positions in borders, edging and planting in rock gardens and sink gardens. They are also available as standards and climbers.

Species and Shrub Roses There are great opportunities for adorning modern gardens with species and shrub roses. Many, such as *Rosa moyesii*, with its profusion of deep red blossoms, followed by large, bottle-shaped red hips, and the *R. spinossissima* hybrid, 'Frühlingsgold', which is smothered

with yellow flowers in May, are too large for most gardens, but there are other more modest growers that can be planted as specimens in the lawn or among shrubs, as can the very beautiful *rugosa* shrubs, clear rose-pink 'Fraü Dagmar Hastrup', deep crimson 'Mrs Anthony Waterer', and the velvety, dark crimson, almost black, *gallica* shrub, 'Tuscany Superb'. There are also modern shrub roses that flower twice and are not too large. These include the Kordes shrub roses, apricot-yellow 'Grandmaster', light crimson 'Elmshorn', and blood red 'Kassel', and the hybrid musk roses, 'Cornelia' and 'Felicia'. More recently developed are 'The David Austin New English Roses', which include among them the diminutive shrub type roses, crimson and purple 'The Knight' and warm pink 'The Wife of Bath', both under 2 ft. in height.

Rose Hedges An excellent way of enjoying roses, particularly in a small garden, is to make a hedge of them. Suitable ones for this purpose are the white *rugosa*, 'Blanc Double de Coubert' (about 4 ft.), the hybrid musk, 'Penelope' (5 ft.), the floribunda – hybrid tea type, pink – 'Queen Elizabeth' (6–8 ft.) and the hybrid tea rose,

The scarlet, sweetly-scented blooms of the recurrent-flowering climber 'Copenhagen' are best against a wall

'Peace' ($4\frac{1}{2}$ ft.).
Climbing Roses The old-fashioned ramblers, such as 'Dorothy Perkins' and 'American Pillar', were once much cherished, but, because they flower once only in the summer (admittedly with a glorious display) and are so vigorous that it is essential that they are pruned and tied in immediately after they have flowered, present-day gardeners have little time for them. Fortunately, since 1930, when the pale flesh-pink, once-flowering 'Dr W. van Fleet', threw a sport, 'New Dawn', which was of the same colour, recurrent-flowering, but far less vigorous, there has been bred from it a range of modern climbing roses, which are very suitable for present-day conditions.

Among the roses that have stemmed from 'New Dawn' are 'Bantry Bay', 'Parade' and 'Schoolgirl'. The German hybridist Wilhelm Kordes has been responsible for raising another very attractive group of climbers, known as the Kordes climbers or pillar roses.

Sedum

Butterfly or Ice Plant

The taller herbaceous sedums include such well-established favourites as *S. spectabilis*, 1–1½ ft. tall, with wide heads densely packed with glistening pink flowers in late summer. The varieties 'Brilliant', 'Carmen' and 'Meteor' do not differ greatly from one another. 'Autumn Joy', 2 ft., is a sturdy plant with heads up to 12–15 in. across, opening light pink in September, changing slowly to salmon-rose. *S. heterodontum*, 9–12 in., is another easy, somewhat fleshy-rooted, compact plant with fuzzy heads of a burnt orange

Sedum spectabile

colour and bluish foliage. The yellow-flowered *S. rhodiola*, the rose root sedum, is of a similar dwarf bushy habit. Plants are easily divided.

Sedum (Crassulaceae) (Stone Crop)
Many of these easy, sun-loving plants are decorative for the rock garden.

Shrubs

Raising your Own Shrubs (and Trees)
Shrubs, and still more so trees, are the most expensive items in the plant world of the gardener. This is principally because they take much longer to produce than, for example, bedding out plants or perennials. Furthermore, the nurseryman, for commercial reasons, raises only things for which there is a regular popular demand, whereas the gardener may want something, say a tree that he has seen in a friend's garden, which he cannot find in any nurseryman's list or displayed at any garden centre.

Propagation by Layering Few shrubs are more desirable or more expensive than magnolias. These are quite easily reproduced by layering – as are rhododendrons. As it does little harm to an established plant, you can generally get a friend to let you operate on one that you covet. Spring is the best time to carry out the operation but any time of the year will do. You choose a low-lying shoot and remove the leaves from its base. You then lightly fork the soil below it, working in some peat. Then scrape away the soil and gently pull down the shoot into the hollow. When it is firmly embedded, you either by means of a stout wire hook driven into the ground or a good heavy stone laid on it, fix the shoot, firmly pressing it into the ground. And firm it must be, for your next operation is to bend the free end upwards as steeply as you can

and tie it firmly to a stout stake that has been driven in beside it. Then cover the base of the shoot with peaty soil and press it down firmly.

Next you wait for a season's growth to take place, i.e., for a year after the layering. Then cut through the junction of your layered shoot with the main plant and, after cutting the ties to the stake, very carefully, with a fork, remove the layer, which should have produced roots (which must not

Above: Genista cinerea, *a good broom for dry soils*

be broken).

Sometimes the layered plant will have grown bigger and will be so well rooted that it can go into its final place at once. Otherwise it should be planted in a nursery bed and left there for a further year before it is again lifted and planted in its permanent position.

Most shrubs that have low-sweeping branches – particularly, as already mentioned, rhododendrons, can be propagated in this way. In fact, if you look and feel carefully round the base of an old rhododendron bush you may find naturally self-layered pieces which can be carefully cut away, forked up, and planted (preferably in autumn) with plenty of peat worked into the fine root system. Layered plants must be well staked when put into their final position as the fine roots formed are only surface roots.

Propagation by Cuttings A great many trees and shrubs can be quite easily propagated from cuttings. All poplars (*populus*) and all willows (*salix*) grow freely from stout shoots cut in winter when they are dormant. Once the ground where they are to grow perma-

Above: 'Royal Red' a fine variety of Buddleia davidii

nently has been cleaned and dug, they are driven in and the soil round them firmed, a stout tool being used to make a hole to receive them. They should be firmly staked. The shoots from the lower part of the sett – for this is what these stout cuttings are called – should be cut clean back to the stem. Very considerable branches of the popular weeping willow can be propagated in this way and a substantial tree can be produced in a few years. As a general rule willow cuttings need a moist situation.

Pruning Shrubs When we come to the pruning of shrubs, certain main principles apply. One reason for pruning is to tidy up the shrub. Another is to prevent overcrowding of its stems. There are, however, two main rules to follow when shrub pruning. Firstly, it is important to remember that some kinds flower mostly on wood that was produced and ripened in the past year; that wood must be retained.

Secondly, a considerable number flower on shoots that have grown during the current year – that is, you cut them hard back early in the spring. So take some advice before you set to work with the secateurs.

The craft of pruning is most easily learned by seeing examples of it that have been well done. Today, so often (but not always) this is carried out in local parks, visits to which are always worthwhile. Always use sharp secateurs and well-sharpened pruning saws.

Spinach

Spinach (Summer Spinach) (Round-seeded Spinach)

Sow seeds in mid-March and make

successional sowings until July.

Sow in 1-in. deep drills, 1 ft. apart and thin seedlings to 3 in. Keep plants well watered in dry weather. Harvest but a few leaves from each plant at any one picking.

Spinach (Winter Spinach) (Prickly-seeded Spinach)

Sow and cultivate as summer spinach but wait until July or August before sowing. Cloches come in handy for protecting the plants during the winter.

Strawberries

The Care of Strawberries

Weeds must be kept down in the strawberry bed but any hoeing must be very shallow to avoid root damage: it is better to use paraquat/diquat weed-killer whenever possible, being very careful not to let it touch the leaves of the strawberry plants.

When the berries begin to swell take steps to prevent soil-splashes spoiling

Above: 'Gento' will yield strawberries between June and October

them. There are three ways, the traditional one being to spread a little clean straw over the soil and beneath the fruit trusses. Alternatively buy proprietary strawberry mats and lay one of these round each plant, or put down black polythene tucking it into the soil or weighting it down with stones to prevent the wind getting beneath it. Never put straw or other mulches down too early as they may increase the risk of frost damage to open flowers.

Quite early in the season summer-fruiting strawberries start trying to propagate their kind by producing runners – cord-like growths on which tiny plants develop. These should always be cut off as soon as seen unless you wish to raise new plants. Unless you are very sure that your strawberries are quite free from virus disease infection (to which they are extremely prone) it is wiser to leave propagation to the experts and buy new plants as required. It is never advisable to keep a strawberry bed for more than three seasons.

If you decide to raise your own plants, simply sink a 3-in. pot of good growing compost (John Innes potting compost or soilless compost) into the ground by the parent plant where the plantlet on the runner can be bent down. Hold the runner in place with a stone or 'hairpin' of galvanized wire

you force a few pots in the greenhouse. 'Royal Sovereign' and 'Grandee' are good varieties for this. Early-rooted runners are needed for this purpose – late July if possible. Plant in 9-in. pots using J.I.P.3 potting compost. Stand the pots in the open on a sheet of polythene until mid-November and then either turn them on their sides (to prevent over-watering) or put them in a cold frame. Towards the end of January transfer to an unheated greenhouse. When fresh growth becomes visible, start watering cautiously and turn on the artificial heat. A night tem-

nels at the end of February. Deal with all weeds before covering. Keep closed until the blossom opens and then open cloches or pull them apart slightly and open tunnels fully by day to allow entry of pollinating insects. Close tunnels and cloches again by 4 p.m. In April and May ventilate in sunny weather to prevent a dangerously high build-up of temperature. In dry weather watering may be necessary. Do this in the morning to let the plants dry before ventilation is closed again.

Perpetual-fruiting Kinds These need slightly different treatment. In the first

Above: To save space strawberries may be grown decoratively in a barrel

Right: Strawberry 'Royal Sovereign', one of the most popular varieties. It bears fruit in early or mid-summer

and pinch out the tip of the runner to prevent further growth. At the end of July the new plant can be separated from its parent and a week or two later lifted and replanted.

As soon as picking is finished, cut all the old leaves off with shears and deal with any weeds. In early autumn rake in ½ oz. per sq. yd. each of sulphate of ammonia and sulphate of potash and put down a mulch of well-rotted farm or stable manure or garden compost (about 5 lb. per sq. yd.).

Greenhouse Culture The strawberry season can begin very much sooner if

perature of 45°F (7°C) will be quite sufficient at first. Let this rise gradually to 50°F (10°C) when the blossom trusses are seen. Pollinate the flowers by hand, dusting their centres with a camel's-hair brush. When the blossom has fallen the night temperature may be permitted to rise another five degrees to 55°F (13°C) and gentle liquid feeding should begin and be continued until the berries colour.

Cloches and Tunnels The strawberry season can also be advanced two or three weeks by covering first-year plants with cloches or polythene tun-

season, nip off all flower trusses which appear before June. In subsequent years all blossom may be allowed to develop. Some do not produce runners freely; where new plantlets appear they may be allowed to root and may flower and fruit the same season. After fruiting the first year cut off all old leaves but in subsequent years leave them to fall naturally. Always burn strawberry leaves after removal.

Your Strawberry Choice

Summer-fruiting Varieties Cambridge Vigour (First-early); very early in maiden year, thereafter mid-season.

Good for cloching in first year. Good cropper. Juicy berries with good flavour. Cambridge Rival (First-early): good for cloching. Erect foliage suits wet land. Good flavour. Cambridge Favourite (Second-early): good for cloching. Very heavy cropper. Little flavour. Gorella (Second-early): very heavy cropper. Berries large but uneven shape. Not very sweet. Moderate flavour. Grandee (Second-early): outstanding for size of berry, particularly in second season. Crops heavily but berries will not travel. First-class flavour. Royal Sovereign (Early mid-season): The 'Rolls-Royce' of strawberries but does not crop heavily and very susceptible to disease. Good for forcing. Domanil (Late mid-season): very heavy cropper. Fair flavour, somewhat acid. Elista (Late mid-season): very heavy cropper but not outstanding flavour. Excellent for jamming. Plants are small and can be planted only 9 in. apart. Flowers after frosts. Red Gauntlet (Late mid-season: heavy cropper. Large, dark crimson berries. Little flavour. Cambridge Late Pine (Late): frost-resistant. Fair cropper. Very good flavour and recommended for bottling. Talisman (Late): heavy cropper and very vigorous. Good flavour. May produce second crop in October.

Perpetual-fruiting Variety Gento: now thought by many to be the best of this class. First trusses may ripen in June. Yields well with heaviest crop between August and October. Large berries of very good flavour.

Alpine Varieties Baron Solemacher: larger berries than wild strawberries and less acid than the cultivated summer strawberries. Does not produce runners. Rich flavour. Alexandria and Delicious: improved strains of Baron Solemacher with larger berries and better disease resistance. Alpine Yellow: golden yellow berries with excellent flavour.

Swede

Swede 'Purple-Top' is a popular swede. Very new and noted for resistance to club root (see The Cabbage Tribe) is 'Chignecto'. Sow seed in early June.
Sowing Sow thinly in 1-in. deep drills spaced at 18 in. apart. Hoe to prevent weeds from developing. Thin seedlings to 1 ft. apart. Pull swedes for use in autumn/early winter. Any swedes not used by Christmas should be pulled up and stored in the same way as carrots.

Sweet Corn
Corn on the Cob

Sow two or three seeds in 3½-in. pots in a greenhouse or cold frame in late April. Thin the seedlings to leave one only in each pot. Plant out in early June in blocks consisting of several plants about 1 ft. apart. Harvest cobs when the grains are full but immature in August. At that stage the 'silks' hanging from the cobs are dark brown to black in colour and brittle.

Inspecting sweet corn for ripeness

Sweet Peas

A most popular annual, the sweet pea *(Lathyrus odoratus)* is not difficult to grow, though the richer the soil the better the results. Given good cultivation it will produce stems 2 ft. long bearing four, five or more florets. Elegant, graceful and fragrant, with the exception of yellow, it will provide every colour of the spectrum and dozens of different tones or shades. It is a 'cut-and-come-again' annual; indeed, every other day blooms should be gathered to keep the plants in full production.

The 'Spencer' type, trained up canes in 'cordon fashion', will grow to a height of 14 ft. though this means that all side shoots need to be removed during the growing season and every few days there is the business of tying or ringing the thick haulms (stems), and once or twice during the summer kneeing, or layering, is called for. On the other hand, if the sweet pea is allowed to go its own way brushwood or wire to the height of 8 ft. will not be too tall.
Soils Land enriched with farmyard manure at the rate of one barrowful to each strip of 15 ft. by 4 ft., dug in autumn or early winter into the second spit of soil and fortified by ½ lb. of bonemeal, will give the best results, or good garden compost at the same rate will serve.
When to Sow In the North sow from late September to 7th October. In the Midlands and the South, from the 5th to the 21st October. It is best to sow in a shallow frame, otherwise the plants tend to get drawn; the aim is short, stocky plants.
Sowing Six seeds to a 6-in. pot, sown an inch from the edge is ideal; or if boxes are used sow the seeds 2 in. apart each way. Sow ¾ in. deep. Use a moist compost of 3 parts of sieved loam, 1 part of peat and 1 part of coarse sand. Cover the pots or boxes with thick layers of paper to prevent drying out; replace the framelights after placing slug pellets between the pots or boxes. Set a couple of mouse-traps, for mice find the seeds irresistible. Inspect after a week and as soon as the shoots appear remove the paper. Water if necessary,

and after a day or two open up the frames and do not replace the lights unless frost is threatened. In hard or severe frosts keep the lights down and cover them with old carpets or sacks. Never let the sun shine on pots and boxes if the soil within them is frozen, since a quick thaw does great damage to the plants.

Springtime sowing will require a greenhouse. When the plants have four leaves pinch out the growing points to induce side shoots. When these are 1½ in. long, harden off the plants by placing the pots or boxes in a frame or under the south wall of the greenhouse.

For a late spring sowing the seeds may be sown ¾ in. deep, like garden peas. Always put down slug killer.

Planting Never plant out until the soil on the plot has been reduced to a fine tilth. Then erect the canes if the plants are to be grown cordon style. A strong support at each end of each row will be necessary, with a cross-bar at a height of 5 ft. Double rows, 2 ft. apart, are best, as this helps when it is time to layer. Stretch strong wire from the end of each cross-bar, insert 8-ft. tall canes, 7 in. apart, and secure them to the wire Using a trowel, make holes to receive the plants *on the outside* of each cane, to facilitate layering. If the plants are to be in circles, they should be planted *inside* the circle of hazel sticks or brush-wood. If a circle of netting is to be made, plant first and surround with the netting. Spread the roots and return the soil, so that it just covers the white collar of the plant. If a plant has a brown collar, reject it. It may grow to a

Above: Sweet Pea 'Legend'

Left: Sweet Pea 'Bijou Mixed'

height of 3 or 4 ft. and then collapse. Always surround each plant with small twigs. Black cotton stretched across the twigs will deter sparrows.

May is a month of vigorous growth. Cordon plants should by then have been restricted to a solitary stem. This is done by removing the weaker of the side shoots, of which there may be three or more. Tie in the stems in the early stages, very loosely, using raffia. At 1 ft. in height the big sweet pea metal rings may be used for fastening. Pinch out side shoots and tendrils to channel the sap into the one stem.

When the plants are grown 'naturally' side shoots are left alone and the tendrils are not removed.

Watering Never allow the land or the plants to become dry. Water the former and spray the latter.

Choosing Varieties The most popular sweet pea is the 'Spencer' which grows tall, has exceptionally long stems, and carries 4–6 florets per stem. 'Galaxy Hybrids', also tall-growing, will carry as many as nine or more florets per stem, but they are not so nicely placed. The shorter type known as 'Knee-Hi' grows into a nice bush, needs little support, and will reach a height of 4½ ft. with flower stems about 1 ft. long. Some dwarf types are less useful if cut-blooms are required; 'Little Sweetheart' varieties grow to 1 ft. and 'Colour Carpet' 6 in. 'Bijou' and 'Dwarf Pigmy' will sometimes grow to a height of 3 ft. but the flower stems are short.

The following is a list of 'Spencer' sweet peas including good exhibition varieties and types suitable for decorative purposes, chosen from hundreds of named varieties. Where two or three of the same colour are named there is not much to choose between them.

White: 'White Leamington'; 'White Ensign'; 'Majesty'.
Cream: 'Hunter's Moon'; 'Margot'.
Picotee: 'Selana'; 'Tell Tale'.
Pale Blue: 'Cambridge'; 'Larkspur'.
Mid-Blue: 'Noel Sutton'.
Deep Blue: 'Blue Velvet'.
Lavender: 'Leamington'; 'Harmony'.
Mauve: 'Mauve Leamington'; 'Reward'.
Salmon Pink: (*white ground*) 'Splendour'; 'Superfine'.
Salmon Pink: (*cream ground*) 'Royal Flush'; 'Philip Simons'.
Almond-blossom Pink: 'Southbourne'.
Orange-Cerise: 'Herald'; 'Clarion'; 'Alice Hardwick'.
Scarlet: 'Firebrand'.

Tools for the Garden

One could very quickly fill the garden shed with a massive array of garden tools and the very wide range of equipment which is available today is very tempting.

There are several basic tools with which most of the essential and basic routine garden work can be carried out. It is a simple matter to add to a basic collection from time to time.

The backbone of any collection of equipment is the digging spade and fork. Unless selected with a little care, these two tools can be uncomfortable and tiring to use. Look for a comfortable handle or grip. The latest designs are made from plastics which are smooth and very comfortable. If possible, go through the motions of digging, in the shop or garden centre and *do* select a spade or fork which is *not* heavy for you personally. Good balance is another useful buying point. Although the beautiful stainless steel tools reduce effort, especially in the wet or heavier soils, they are quite expensive and one of a good untreated steel will prove just as useful – but do keep the tools clean.

There are smaller editions of the digging spade and fork known as the border spade and fork. The working heads (blade or tines) are much smaller and generally the two tools are lighter to handle. They can be used for general work but are especially useful for cultivating in between plants.

Another essential tool is the rake. Try to purchase one which has at least 10 teeth. The more teeth there are the better the finish or breakdown of the soil which can be achieved. Many teeth will also ensure easier and better coverage of seeds and seed drills. Thorough cross-raking of the soil surface will produce a better breakdown of large soil particles and will ensure a finer finish.

There are many different hoe designs. While a draw hoe is very useful for taking out seed drills and for earthing-up operations, the Dutch hoe is essential for keeping down weeds. A useful variant of the Dutch hoe is one which has two serrated cutting edges and this can be used with a push-pull action.

A wheelbarrow can play an essential part in the routine garden work and be kept busy throughout the year. Several types of wheelbarrows are available with large or small capacities. One of lightweight yet strong design with two wheels is highly manouverable. The sloping front and closeness to the ground enables the user to tip it forward and sweep debris into it.

A length of good quality hose will be required for watering in and around the garden. There are new designs available now with specially strengthened walls which withstand high water pressures. It is very important that a hose pipe is stored correctly, otherwise it becomes kinked and splits may occur. The purchase of a hose reel or holder will be a sound investment.

The correct application of water is important also and a sprinkler will ensure this. Many different versions are on the market and these provide coverages which will suit the small garden or the very large one. An oscillating sprinkler is a very efficient versatile type. It can be set to water different areas or patterns and thoroughly soaks the ground.

Pruning is an important task and a good pair of secateurs is essential. There are heavy-duty models which will deal with quite tough wood as well as lightweight models which can be conveniently slipped into the pocket. Normally, a general purpose type which is strong enough to deal with a wide variety of woods and thicknesses will be adequate.

For planting large specimens such as trees, shrubs, etc., the spade can be used, but for smaller plants a hand trowel and fork should be used. A stainless steel pair would be a good investment. Comfortable, smooth handles are important.

Pest and disease control depends a lot on efficient spraying equipment. The capacity of the sprayer should be closely considered and for the larger garden the compression or pressure sprayer is most suitable.

Tomato 'Outdoor Girl'

Tomatoes

These vary very much in shape and size. 'Big Boy' averages from 8–12 oz. each; 'Sugarplum' (Gardener's Delight) measures no more than 1 in. in diameter. Most varieties produce tomatoes weighing 8 or 9 to the pound. Red is the usual colour; white is rare, but yellow tomatoes, e.g. 'Tangella', are liked by some gardeners. 'Tigerella' and 'Tiger Tom' are red tomatoes with yellow striping.

Most plants are grown as single cordons; there are also self-stopping bush varieties such as 'The Amateur'. Varieties were and still are usually bred for greenhouse cultivation; 'Outdoor Girl' (a cordon) and the dwarf bush tomatoes are for open garden cultivation only.

Sowing Sow seeds in the greenhouse in late February or March in a temperature of 65°F (18°C), dropping a few degrees lower at night. In the south of England sow seeds in an unheated greenhouse in early April. Slight heat is needed elsewhere. For plants to be moved into the garden later, sow in early April.

Sow seeds about 1 in. apart in J.I. seed compost or soilless compost and cover with more compost. Firm gently, water thoroughly and cover with a sheet of glass and lay a sheet of brown paper over it. Turn the glass daily to rid it of excess moisture. As soon as germination is seen, remove the glass and paper. Two to three weeks later pot the seedlings into 3½-in. pots. Always hold seedlings by a seed leaf, never by the stem. A night temperature of at least 56°F (13°C) is best.

In the greenhouse border space the plants 18 in. apart and tie them as they grow to stout bamboo canes. The soil should be well drained and enriched with partially rotted strawy manure or garden compost. Plants must never be short of water. Good ventilation is necessary. Side shoots must be pinched out frequently, when they are small. When the plants have attained their full height, nip out the growing point.

There are four other ways of growing tomatoes in a greenhouse:
(1) *In Pots* Plants may be grown successfully in large pots filled with a suitable compost, housed on the greenhouse staging.

Tomatoes in the greenhouse.
Left: 'Tom-Bags';
Centre: 'Ring culture' method;
Right: Plants grown in straw bales

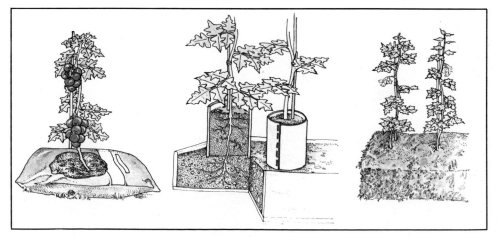

(2) *Ring Culture* Soil in the borders is removed to a depth of 6 in. and replaced by an aggregate (sieved clinker, ash or screened, washed, coarse gravel). Plants are grown in clay, plastic or whalehide 'rings', which allow the roots to grow easily into the aggregate.
(3) *Straw Bale* A 56 lb. bale of wheat straw will take two tomato plants. Lay bales in position on the greenhouse border and sprinkle a gallon of water on to each bale every day for 12 days. Then apply to each bale: 1 lb. of Nitro-chalk, 1 lb. of potassium nitrate, $\frac{1}{2}$ lb. of triple superphosphate of lime, $\frac{1}{4}$ lb. of magnesium sulphate (Epsom salts), 3 oz. of sulphate of iron. Water these chemicals in well. Fermentation of the straw occurs in a heated greenhouse and plants are set out in the fermenting straw when the temperature within the bales falls to 100°F (37°C).
(4) *The Tom-bag System* Bags filled with a suitable compost are laid down and panels of the bag are removed and one plant is set in each of the spacings. Using any of these methods it is necessary to feed with a tomato fertilizer.

Although many varieties are capable of ripening fruits in gardens of Southern England, gardeners elsewhere should choose a hardy variety such as 'Outdoor Girl' or 'The Amateur'. Harden off plants before moving them from a greenhouse to the open garden. Plants to be grown under cloches may be moved directly from the greenhouse to where they are to grow. Plant standard tomatoes 15 in. apart with 30 in. between rows and push a bamboo cane alongside each one or erect a simple wire trellis to which plants may be tied periodically. Allow bush plants 2 sq. ft. of soil surface; no staking is necessary. Keep plants watered in dry weather, hoe to keep down weeds, de-shoot standard plants and stop them during the first week of August by pinching out the growing point.

Always leave tomatoes on the plants until they are really ripe. Pick unripe fruits on outdoor plants in late September; the larger fruits will ripen quickly in a warm room indoors. Small green tomatoes are excellent for chutney.

Tomato leaf mould, a fungal disease, is common on greenhouse tomato plants. Yellowish spots appear on the leaves with a pale greyish mould on the underside of the leaves. The foliage dies and the disease passes from plant to plant rapidly. Hot, moist conditions favour the disease. Take care not to over-water, and provide ample ventilation. Never water in the evening. Pick off and burn infected leaves. If the outbreak is severe spray with a copper-based fungicide. Many new varieties resist this disease.

Tomato plants can suffer from several different disorders. Almost always they are caused by faulty cultivation. Should flowers fall without fruits setting it may be that the plants are not receiving sufficient water. Over-watering or irregular watering are two possible causes of blossom end rot, which shows as a dark green patch at the blossom end of the fruit. The patch changes to brown or black and has a leathery texture. If the greenhouse temperature is very high but the soil itself is on the cold side the tomatoes may not ripen well, a condition known as blotchy ripening. Very strong sunlight can lead to a disorder known as greenback. The stalk end stays green or yellow but the rest of the tomato ripens well. Some varieties never suffer from greenback. These are catalogued as 'greenback-free'. Potato blight can attack outdoor-grown tomato plants, more often in the wetter, western half of Britain. If, because of blight, the growing of outdoor tomatoes is difficult, be prepared to spray regularly from July to September with Bordeaux mixture or a copper-based fungicide.

Trees
A *deciduous* tree or shrub is one that is bare of leaves in winter. The individual leaves on an *evergreen* tree or shrub have a life of more than a year, even up to three of four, before they fall.
Standards Most deciduous trees such as crab-apples, cherries and rowans are supplied as standards. That is, in the nursery they are trained up on single bare stems (or leg) with a bunch of shoots at the top. The stems are about 5 ft. high, and are kept clean by prun-

Prunus domestica

ing away side growths. Among the cluster of branches there should be one, somewhere near its centre, which is growing vigorously and is forming a *leader*. This branch should not be cut back, as it is the key to a well-formed crown or head to the young tree.

Half-standards Trees on a stem about half the length of a standard, are sometimes produced and can be most useful.

Planting Assuming that you have decided where to plant your trees or shrubs, you may obtain them in two ways:

First, if they are ordered from a nurseryman they will arrive carefully packed during the dormant season – that is at any time when the leaves have fallen, if they are deciduous trees or shrubs. If they are evergreen trees or shrubs, say conifers or rhododendrons, they will come when growth has apparently ceased – preferably in autumn or early spring. That is still the most usual method followed in supplying trees; the plant is very carefully lifted from the ground by skilled labour and packed so that it will stand the rigours and delays of modern transport on its way to the recipient.

There is now another method, that of 'instant' trees (or shrubs) when the buyer selects his plants growing in containers in the nursery and takes them home to plant without delay.

Planting Standard Trees A start can be made in the autumn. The ground should be deeply forked over and such things as the roots of nettles and docks pulled out. If the ground is very light, compost may be forked in; if it is heavy, some peat will help. For the actual planting, you will need to have some moist peat ready and a good, stout pointed stake, say from 4–5 ft. long, with a supply of the specially designed tree-ties and some string.

If the tree arrives by rail or road, loosen the packing. But do not attempt to plant if there is *any* frost in the ground, or if the ground is saturated. Leave the package in an unheated shed. If conditions for planting are suitable, completely unpack the tree. If deciduous, disentangle the roots, cutting off cleanly any that are broken; if it is a conifer the roots will be in a ball of soil – do not disturb this too much. Dig a hole in the prepared spot of ground wide enough to take the roots spread out, and deep enough to take the tree to the previous depth of

planting, easily identified on the stem by the soil mark, to be as near as possible to that of the present level of the surface. Now drive a stake in, carefully avoiding damage to the roots, as near to the stem of the tree as possible and loosely tie the stem to it. Then start filling in the hole; it is a good thing to sprinkle plenty of moist peat on the roots. Firm the soil by treading gently on it, and before the hole is full, give the tree a good soaking. Then use a tree-tie to replace the string. This can be done single-handed, but a second person to hold the young tree in place, is a great help.

Firmness and stability are the secrets of tree and shrub planting. The adjustable tree-ties must be examined, say, twice a year. The stake can be removed when it is obvious that the trees are firmly anchored.

The treatment for 'instant' trees and conifers is much the same, but here you have the roots carefully grown in a ball, which must not be broken. Staking is just as important, if indeed not more so. Regular watering for at least the first season after planting is essential, for it is easy for the ball of roots to dry out and it is difficult to wet it properly once this has happened.

Pruning Trees As far as the pruning of ornamental trees is concerned the objective is to produce nice, shapely specimens that look attractive even when bare of leaves. We grow these to become standards, that is, to have a crown of branches on top of a clean stem or trunk, perhaps 6 ft. or more tall. All side shoots on this stem must, therefore, be removed. But the leading shoot, the natural growing point, must not be cut back. We want to aim for a stem – eventually the trunk – arising from ground level and carrying through gracefully to the top of the tree. It is an aim that admittedly cannot always be fulfilled, as, for example, the upper part of crab apples generally and unavoidably becomes a bit of a tangle. But growth should always spread from the top of a clean stem.

As to the actual operation of pruning, the main objective is to make as clean a cut as possible, close up to the stem (but not damaging it) so that the bark can gradually spread over and heal the wound. Do not let the piece

Acer palmatum, the Japanese maple

you are cutting off come away and tear bark with it. If the shoot you are cutting off is stout and heavy, shorten it first so as to avoid its weight tearing it away. If the wound you leave is large – say an inch or more in diameter – it is as well to paint it with one of the special proprietary paints. Infection can quickly take hold, particularly in the growing season.

Suckers coming up from the bottom of a tree must always be removed; it is quite possible that they come from the quite different stock on which your tree was grafted or budded.

When two branches have grown together so that they rub the least important must be removed.

When it comes to dealing with large branches on big trees, it is essential to leave this to a qualified tree surgeon. It needs most careful judgement to effect a good job and can be dangerous to an unskilled operator as well as, perhaps, causing damage to passers-by or neighbouring property.

Tulip
Tulipa (Lily family)
Tulips have been favourite spring bedding and pot plants in Europe since the mid-16th century. The flowers are in all colours except true blues, usually solitary, but also 3–4 per stem, the garden hybrids ranging in height from 4–34 in. Good bulbs can be guaranteed to give a fine, even display the first season, but except in warm situations on sandy loam rarely produce so many or such large blooms in later years, though feeding with bonemeal and proper ripening do help, and by this treatment the smaller species may become established on sunny ledges of the rock garden. The bulbs should be planted from 4–6 in. deep according to their size, but should not be put in before October for the April flowering kinds and November for the May flowering ones.

If used for spring bedding, either alone or coming through a shorter ground cover of forget-me-nots, wallflowers or pansies, the bulbs will have to be lifted and allowed to finish their growth in trenches in a sunny position, unless discarded. Tulips in less conspicuous places should be allowed to die down before being lifted and placed in trays in a sunny place (cold greenhouse, frame or window) to complete their ripening. Only the large bulbs

117

should be planted for display the following year, but the small ones can be grown on to flowering size in a sunny frame. They take up to seven years to flower from seed.

Some varieties can be forced, but it is very important to grow the bulbs in a plunge bed until growth is well up (4–6 in.) and then to bring them gradually into light and moderate warmth. They do not respond well to high temperatures and must be forced slowly.

Right: 'Rosy Wings', a Cottage tulip. Far right: Tulip 'Carl M Bellman'

Tulip species	Height in in.	Flowering time	Flower colour	Use
Acuminata (cornuta) (Horned tulip)	20	May	Yellow, streaked red, long twisted petals	As cut flower, pots
Batalinii	7	April	Primrose or yellow flushed pink	Rock garden or pans
Clusiana (Lady tulip)	15	Late April	Outer petals cherry, inner ones white, violet base	Border or rock garden
Eichleri	12	March	Scarlet, pointed petals, black base	Pots, border
Fosteriana	10–18	Mid-April	Scarlet, crimson within, black base, broad petals, large flower	Princeps 10 in. borders Red Emperor 18 in. pots
Geigii	9	April–May	Scarlet or orange, base black ringed yellow. Leaves mottled with chocolate, flat	Borders, pots, as edging to beds, as leaves are decorative
Kaufmanniana (Water-lily tulip)	8	March–April	Large, cream tinged pink outside, white or cream inside	Fine garden tulip
Linifolia	8	April–May	Scarlet, violet base; leaves narrow, red-edged, wavy margins, flat on soil	High in rock garden to show red stems
Orphanidea	10	March–April	Orange shaded bronze and green yellow base, pointed petals	Rock garden
Praestans 'Fusilier'	10	Early April	Vermilion, 4–6 on a stem	Pot plant, rock garden
Pulchella violacea	4	February–March	Reddish purple, cup-shaped, base black or yellow	Alpine house, rock garden
Saxatillis	10	April	1–3 on a stem, pale lilac, yellow base. Flowers best if crowded	Confine in sunny bed by slates as spreads rapidly, by stolons. Leafs early
Tarda (dasystemon)	6	April	3–6 on a stem, white, yellow inside	Rock garden, in paving pockets, edging beds
Turkestanica	9	February–March	5–9 on a stem, white, orange centres	Rock garden, alpine house

Turnips

There are two main classes. Early turnips for summer and autumn use are quick growers but do not store well. Examples are 'Early Snowball', 'White Milan' and 'Tokyo Cross'. 'Early Green Top Stone' and 'Manchester Market' are two good storing main-crop turnips. 'Hardy Green Round' is the turnip to choose for an abundant supply of 'turnip tops'.

Sowing Sow quick growers at any time between mid-March and July, sow maincrop in mid-July, and to have turnip tops in winter and the following spring, sow seeds in August. Sow seeds in 1-in. deep seed drills spaced at 1 ft. apart. Try not to sow too thickly. Weed and water often in hot, dry weather. Thin seedlings of summer turnips to leave strong plants at from 4–6 in. apart; thin maincrop turnips to 9 in. apart. Do not thin seedlings of turnips being grown solely for the edible foliage ('tops'). Flea beetles make holes in leaves of many seedlings – cabbage, radish, cauliflower, wallflower, alyssum, iberis and turnip. Damage is usually serious if seedlings are left to become dry at the roots. Frequent waterings lead to quicker growth and the seedlings recover from beetle damage. Dusting with derris at weekly intervals helps to control this pest. Strong growing seedlings, although holed by these beetles, do not appear inconvenienced.

Pull summer turnips when they are quite young and tender. Leave winter turnips in the ground and harvest as and when wanted. If you wish, you may lift all remaining turnips in December and store as carrots. When pulling turnip tops try not to take more than a couple of leaves at any one time from each plant.

Unusual Vegetables

Aubergine (Egg Plant)

Sow seeds in pots in a warm greenhouse in late April. Plant out in the greenhouse border in late May, or grow the plants in large pots in a greenhouse or cold frame. Pinch out the central growing point of established plants to encourage sub-lateral shoots. Water

Left: Aubergine 'Black Pekin' a variety of the egg plant

Right: Sweet red pepper 'Bull Nosed Red'

Below: The edible swollen stems of kohl rabi should be harvested when no larger than a cricket ball

well and spray with tepid water occasionally to prevent red spider infestation. Harvest the purple, egg-shaped fruits when they are glossy and softening.

Capsicum or *Sweet Pepper*

Sow in small pots in a greenhouse at a minimum temperature of 60°F (15°C) in March or April. Plants may be grown in a greenhouse, either in the border or in large pots, or transferred to cold frames. Allow 18 in. between plants. Keep them well watered.

Chervil (Turnip-Rooted Chervil)

Sow in April and cultivate as parsnips. Dig the roots as and when required in winter, or lift and store in moist sand in October.

Chicory

Sow seeds 1 in. deep in early June and thin seedlings to 9 in. apart. In November dig up the parsnip-like roots and heel them in a trench over which a little straw should be spread. Take small batches for chicon production now and then during the winter. Trim roots back by a few inches and reduce the foliage to within 1 in. of the crown. Plant roots closely in the greenhouse border and cover with straw weighed down with dry soil. Inspect for chicons after a month or so. Alternatively, plant prepared roots in pails or pots and force chicons indoors or in a garage or shed. It is important that all light be excluded.

Courgettes

These are small immature vegetable marrows. 'Zucchini' and 'Courgette' are excellent varieties. Sow and cultivate as bush type marrows. Cut courgettes regularly when they are a few inches long.

Endive

Sow and cultivate as lettuce. Hearts may be partially blanched by tying the plants with string. Full blanching is achieved by covering the plants with large pots so that all light is excluded.

Kohlrabi

Sow at any time between March and August. Thin seedlings to 9 in. apart. The thinnings may be transplanted. Harvest when the turnip-like swollen stems are no larger than a tennis ball.

Pea (Asparagus Pea)

Sow in a shallow drill in late May. Space the seeds at 6 in. apart and thin the young plants to 1 ft. apart. Give the plants some twiggy brushwood supports. Gather the pods when they are about 1 in. long.

Pea (Mangetout or Sugar Pea)

Sow and cultivate as garden peas and provide the plants with supports. Harvest pods before the seeds swell.

Seakale Beet (Swiss Chard, Silver Beet)

Sow seeds in shallow drills 12 in. apart between April and July. Thin seedlings to 12 in. apart. When plants are fully grown pick leaves as required. The thick white midribs may be cooked as a substitute for seakale.

Wallflowers

Cheiranthus (Hardy Biennial) 15 in.
C. X allionii, is the Siberian wallflower with bright orange flowers from March to May. 'Golden Bedder' is a more mellow golden-yellow variety. The common wallflower, *C. cheiri*, $1\frac{1}{2}$ ft. is perennial in some gardens, but both these wallflowers are best treated as biennials and sown in an open seed bed in May, or mid-June for the Siberian wallflower, and transplanted to flowering positions in October. The fragrance of wallflowers on a warm sunny day is glorious and they associate happily with tulips, forget-me-nots and polyanthus. The range of colour is splendid – blood red, scarlet, purple, pink, yellow, ivory white and there is a delightful strain of mixed colours known as 'Persian Carpet'. The 'Tom Thumb' varieties, 9 in. tall in various colours, are admirable for small beds, window boxes or for filling a gap at the front of a border.

The wallflower (Cheiranthus cheiri)

Walls and Steps and Arches

The character and appearance of a garden can be enhanced considerably if features are constructed with decorative stone. Great strides have been made in recent years by manufacturers and a wide range of attractive stone is available for all purposes. Textured surfaces to several types of walling provide the gardener with an opportu-

A corner of a thoughtfully designed paved garden

nity to create a layout which, after a comparatively short period, looks as though it has been established for many years and is, to a certain extent, a natural feature with its slightly uneven or irregular surface.

Several types of bricks for walling have a rough cut surface and give the appearance of having been hewn out of natural stone. Colour has been added to walling materials and this innovation certainly brightens up a patio or terrace – provided the colours are subtle.

Quality walling is expensive but it is a very sound investment. It will add value to the property and will last for many years without the need for maintenance. Selection of sizes, texture and colours is easy because the leading manufacturers provide well-illustrated colour catalogues.

There are several types of walling stone. Some are similar to house bricks in size but much heavier as they are made from reconstituted stone. Screen walling blocks are available with either a solid face and a design in relief on it or with a delicate tracery of pattern. Random walling is also available in several different shapes or sizes. Used in various combinations, a very effective pattern can be built up although much more care and time is required during construction. Flat slabs of stone can be used for dry walling – an in-

triguing system of building walls, between the courses of which suitable plants can be established.

Raised beds add character to a garden design and rough or natural textured bricks and coping stones can be used to construct this type of feature. A raised bed will be appreciated by the elderly or handicapped gardener as it will reduce stooping or bending to a minimum. Furthermore, such raised beds allow gardeners with sight problems to appreciate better the full beauty of the plants.

Steps are essential in a garden which has pronounced levels or which slopes sharply. A combination of bricks and paving slabs will produce a neat effect.

Steps can be built with crazy paving to provide a rustic or natural finish, but a little care is necessary during the work to make sure that all the irregularly shaped pieces are securely seated in their mortar bed.

Retaining Walls Although these are strictly vertical features, they seem to belong with steps and terraces and so find their place here. Retaining walls should usually be made of (or at least faced with) the same material as the house to which they belong. If for some reason this is not possible they should be constructed from local stone or other material, or failing that be designed to be completely hidden by climbing and trailing plants. It is naturally essential that retaining walls should retain, and they must, therefore, be built on very solid foundations and can often be helped by a backing of rough concrete and reinforcing bars. Weep holes must always be left at the base of such walls to prevent water from being trapped behind and undermining the foundations. There was an unfortunate fashion in the earlier years of this century for making stone walls with earth joints in imitation of those retaining the steep-sided lanes in the stone counties. In the cracks were grown suitable plants and ferns but unless they were faultlessly made and maintained they either tended to collapse or become infested with deep-rooted weeds impossible to dislodge without demolishing the wall. Even worse was a fashion for leaving odd holes in the face of walls in order to grow tufts of trailing plants which merely resulted in the face of the wall having a spotty appearance.

The Waste Corner

Many gardens have awkward bits of land, often sloping and dry, perhaps shaded by trees when the sun shines and which drip when it rains. They are spots in which practically none of the ordinary run of garden plants, except a few snowdrops – will thrive.

However, there are several shrubby plants perhaps not considered exciting enough for the garden itself, that will grow quite happily in such places, spreading when once established, and giving quite a lot of interest.

Generally in such places, all that grows naturally is rough grass. To establish plants, patches of this should be killed by spraying with a herbicide. As soon as the grass is killed, this ground is dug over and clumps of the following plants established. As this spot is sure to be dry, water them well until they have taken hold.

First, one would choose the Oregon grape, *Mahonia aquifolium*. This was brought here in 1823 from California, by the plant collector David Douglas. With the typical prickly leaves, which colour well in autumn, its spikes of yellow flowers opening in earliest spring followed by little purple grape-like fruit with a grey bloom, it so excited gardeners that for a few years after its arrival plants were sold at ten guineas a time. Then it was found that it would grow anywhere, spreading freely, and though the plant was just as beautiful, the price tumbled.

Rose of Sharon, *Hypericum calyci-num*, is a low growing evergreen shrub that steadily spreads around by means of runners. Because it will thrive anywhere, under any conditions, it is often pushed into waste corners. If it were a new plant, the large yellow flowers which open at about midsummer would cause it to be all the rage.

In wild, rough places, and often in neglected hedgerows, another shrub, the snowberry, *Symphoricarpos albus* (sometimes called *S. racemosa*) will be found. This, an erect growing, slender, suckering, shrub of about 6 ft., is ideal for wasteland. It is quite common and pheasants are reputed to like the berries. These are fleshy, oval and white, $\frac{1}{2}$ in. or so long, with a sparkling crystalline surface. They are a joy to flower arrangers in autumn, and follow the tiny pink flowers in June and July which one usually notices because of the myriads of bees collecting their nectar.

The dwarf *Cotoneaster dammeri (humifusa)* needs a certain amount of light. This is an evergreen, of dense, twiggy growth with glossy green leaves about $\frac{1}{2}$ in. long; self-sown seedlings often arise. But its value for the garden wasteland is that it lies flat on the ground, its shoots curving to conform with the contours. One plant will very soon cover a square yard and more.

Water Garden Features

There is no doubt that one of the most fascinating features which can be constructed in a garden is one which involves the use of water. Water has its own particular charm and there is a considerable therapeutic effect when one sits beside a pool and watches the antics of the fish or the movement of the water created by a fountain or waterfall.

Little artistry or constructional skill is needed in order to complete a very natural-looking effect. This is mainly due to the versatile range of accessories at the gardener's disposal. The simplest feature is a pool which can be either of formal design or informal. The former is either rectangular or square with straight sides or edges or circular. It can be incorporated in many garden schemes and is particularly useful in a terrace or lawn setting. The informal design has an irregular outline and lends itself to the inclusion of other natural features such as a waterfall or stream which is designed to tumble into it. It is important, therefore, to decide at the outset which type of pool is to be constructed. Two ways in which a pool can be built are by using prefabricated pools or by using plastic liners.

Installation is quite straightforward as all that is necessary is for a hole to be excavated just larger than the unit, and, after stones have been removed, some of the excavated soil is used for backfilling when the unit is in place. Care must be taken to see that there are no large areas of unsupported unit which could be damaged or distorted when the water is added. Water is very heavy!

Plastic liner pools are very successful and if the tougher grades of plastic are used, many years of maintenance and replacement-free service should be provided. Some of these liners are coloured – usually a pleasant blue, while others are reinforced with nylon. One of the toughest and most durable of the liners is Butyl, a rubber-based material of exceptional strength. As it is black it looks more natural than the coloured liners.

None of the plastic or rubber-based liners is easy to use in informal pools if the contours of the pool are complex and to reduce the number of necessary folds and creases when the material is laid over the undulations, the number of contours should be kept to a minimum and should also be as gentle as possible.

A formal pool is quite easy to make from a liner and a careful fold at the corners will be all that is necessary to maintain a reasonably crease-free surface all round the pool.

For all liners, an overlap of material must be allowed for so that it can be taken over the edges of the pool by about 6 in. Material for a pool can be calculated on the basis of length (overall length of the pool, plus twice the maximum depth); width (overall width of the pool, plus twice the maximum depth). Allow about 6 in. at the sides and ends for the overlaps.

Where ledges or shelves are required in the pool to provide different depths of water for the various aquatic plants these must be allowed for as extra measurements. Usually one shelf is adequate all round the sides, about 9–10 in. below the surface of the water. To avoid the necessity for shelves, plant containers can be raised on bricks.

Particular care should be exercised when the excavation for a liner pool is being undertaken, and all stones, etc. must be removed to prevent damage to the liner. The base of the site should be lined with about 1 in. of sand which will serve as a cushion for the liner. The edges of the liner in a formal pool can be concealed very attractively if a row of paving slabs is laid all round. In an informal pool, crazy paving could be used or the edge of the plastic can be hidden or trapped by grass turves. The installation of a liner can be facilitated if, when it is in its approximate position, a *little* water is allowed to run into it. The weight of this water will pull and press the plastic in place and it is a very useful method when an informal pool is being made. The edges of the liner can be retained by several pieces of stone as the water is run in.

Features such as a waterfall can be installed very quickly if a prefabricated unit is used. A stream course can also be introduced easily by the use of preformed units. Several can be arranged to form an intriguing course which could empty into a waterfall basin, which in turn finally empties into the main pool itself.

The movement of water from the pool to the top of a waterfall or stream course is provided by an electric pump.

By means of extra piping and gate valves, a powerful surface pump can be used to provide a fountain effect and a waterfall at the same time.

Window Boxes

Those people without a garden (e.g. flat dwellers) will welcome the opportunity of enjoying plant life by the use of window boxes.

The window box should be thoroughly treated with the horticultural grade of a copper naphthenate wood preservative *before* assembly. Place in position *before* planting; they may be too heavy to move when filled with soil. Cover the drainage holes with broken crocks.

Plant Suggestions

Spring Display Plant one or two centre pieces of blue polyanthus and complete the remainder of the box with hyacinths and forget-me-nots.

Summer Display Use as centre pieces ivy-leaved pelargoniums with a plant of *Grevillea robusta* in between these. These plants will provide an attractive feathery foliage fill-in. The remainder of the box can be planted up with *Verbena venosa*. Another planting scheme can include petunias, *Campanula isophylla* and tuberous begonias. As dot or specimen plants for the centre of the box, use half-standard fuchsias.

Zinnias

(Half-hardy Annual) 9 in.–$2\frac{1}{2}$ ft.

Sow the seed in a warm greenhouse in April. There is nothing to be gained by sowing earlier as seedlings are liable to damp off during a cold spell. Prick out into boxes when quite small, or singly into small pots. Harden off carefully in a cold frame before planting out in full sun and in a rich, well-drained soil in early June. There is a diverse selection from giant-flowered and giant-dahlia-flowered varieties, up to $2\frac{1}{2}$ ft. high, to 'Lilliput' and 'Pompon', 9–12 in. and the American raised 'Thumbelina' only 6 in. high. The range of colour includes scarlet, pink, orange, lavender, yellow and white.

Left: The magnificent water garden at Malahide Castle is rich in colour

The scarlet flowers of one of the half-hardy verbena hybrids, provide brilliant colour at the front of this border

Index

ACKNOWLEDGMENTS
The publishers would like to thank the following organizations and individuals for their kind permission to reproduce the photographs in this book:
A–Z Botanical Collection Ltd. 60; Pat Brindley 68, 69 above; P. R. Chapman 27 below, 28 above; R. J. Corbin 102 below; W. F. Davidson 96 above left, 100 above centre; J. E. Downward 20; Downward and Crowson 12, 16 above right, 17, 18 above right, 32 left, 34, 35 right, 83 above, 86 above, 93, 100 below right, 112 below, 120, 121 above, 125; V. Finnis 23, 45 above left, 63, 100 below left, 107, 124; B. Furner 25, 26, 45 below right, 85 right, 110 above right, 111 right, 112 above; M. Grey 66, 72–73; I. Hardwick 36, 81, 83 below, 109 below left; P. Hunt 8, 22, 28 below, 29 above, 48 left, 56 below, 57, 85 left, 96 above centre, 118; A. Huxley 6 below, 27 above, 48 right, 86 below, 88, 121; G. Hyde 9 above left, 19 right, 35 left, 65, 87, 94; L. Johns 21 above and below; D. J. Kesby 16 below left, 110 above left; Marshall Cavendish 73 right; G. Mazza 71, 74; E. Memmler endpapers, 1; J. Moss 70; F. Perry 62; Pictor International 84; R. Procter 14 left and right, 18 left, 80 above and below, 99, 111 left; Harry Smith Horticultural Photographic Collection 2–3, 4–5, 7, 9 below left and above right, 15, 18 below right, 19 left, 24, 29 below, 30, 31, 32 right, 33, 37, 38–39, 42, 43, 44 left and right, 49, 52, 53 above and below, 54, 55, 56 above, 58 below left and above right, 59, 61, 75, 77, 78, 78–79, 89 above left and right, 89 below, 90, 91, 95, 96–97 centre, 97 above, 98 below left and above right, 101, 102 above left and right, 103, 105 above, 106, 108, 109 above right, 113, 114, 115, 116–117, 119, 122; Spectrum Colour Library 69 below, 92–93; E. Whiting (T. Street-Porter) 64.

PDO 82-0916